Welcome
to
40 Antique Botanical Designs to Color

Ready to relax, de-stress & have some fun?

It's time to let your creative "kid" come out to play! Coloring books aren't just for kids anymore.

We have digitally created 40 black & white sketches from the beautiful antique botanical works of Curtis Botanicals – a magazine publication that began in the late 1700's and ended in the early 1800's. We have painstakingly removed the water spots, foxing and other page damage to make these drawings to color.

Some designs in this book are relatively easy to complete while you may find other designs a bit more intricate and challenging.

You can find the "as found" colored originals on our website at www.BotanicalArtDesigns.com. if you'd like to use them as a beginning reference for coloration.

There is no right or wrong color or design so be as creative or traditional as you'd like. The key is to relax and let your mind focus on your design work.

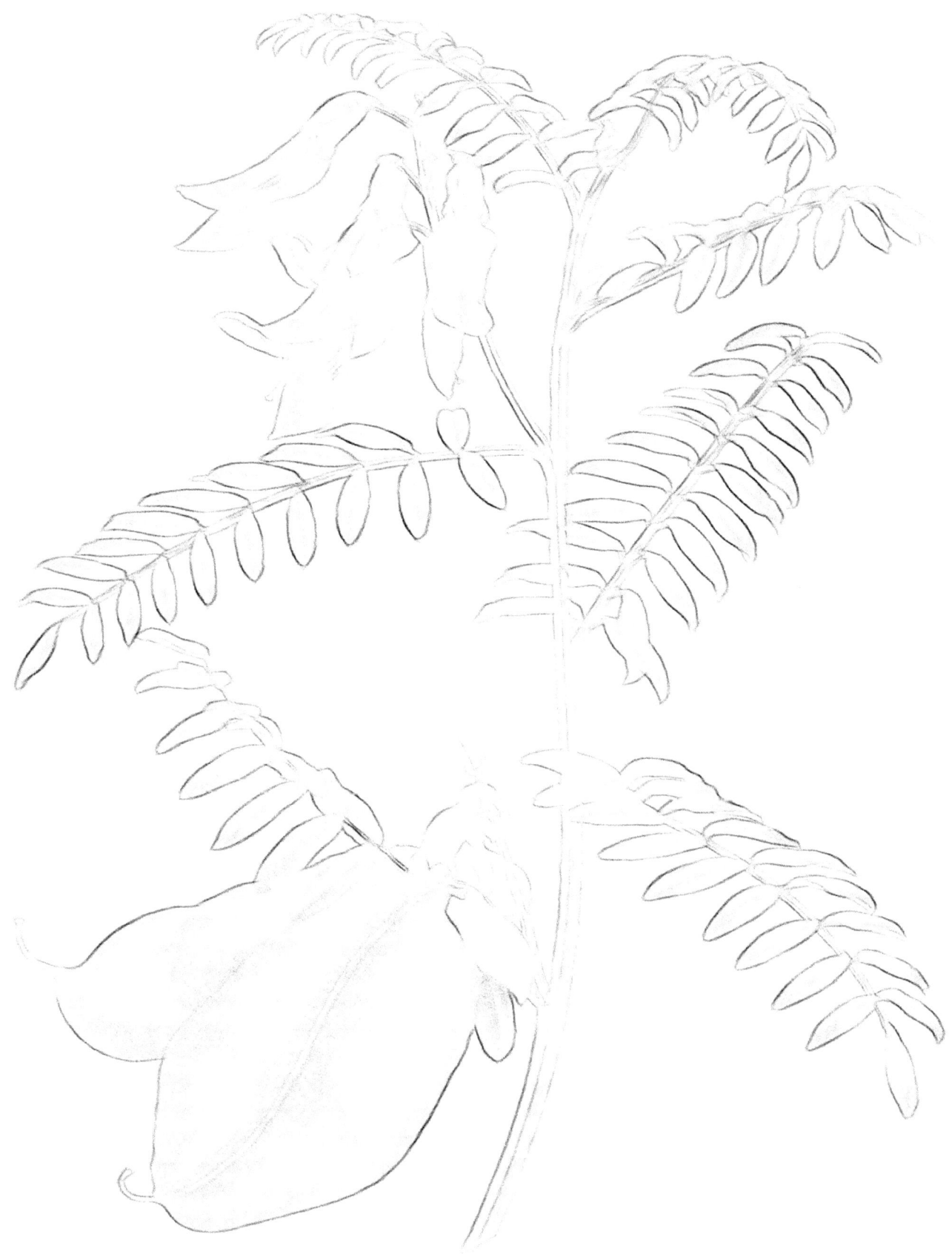

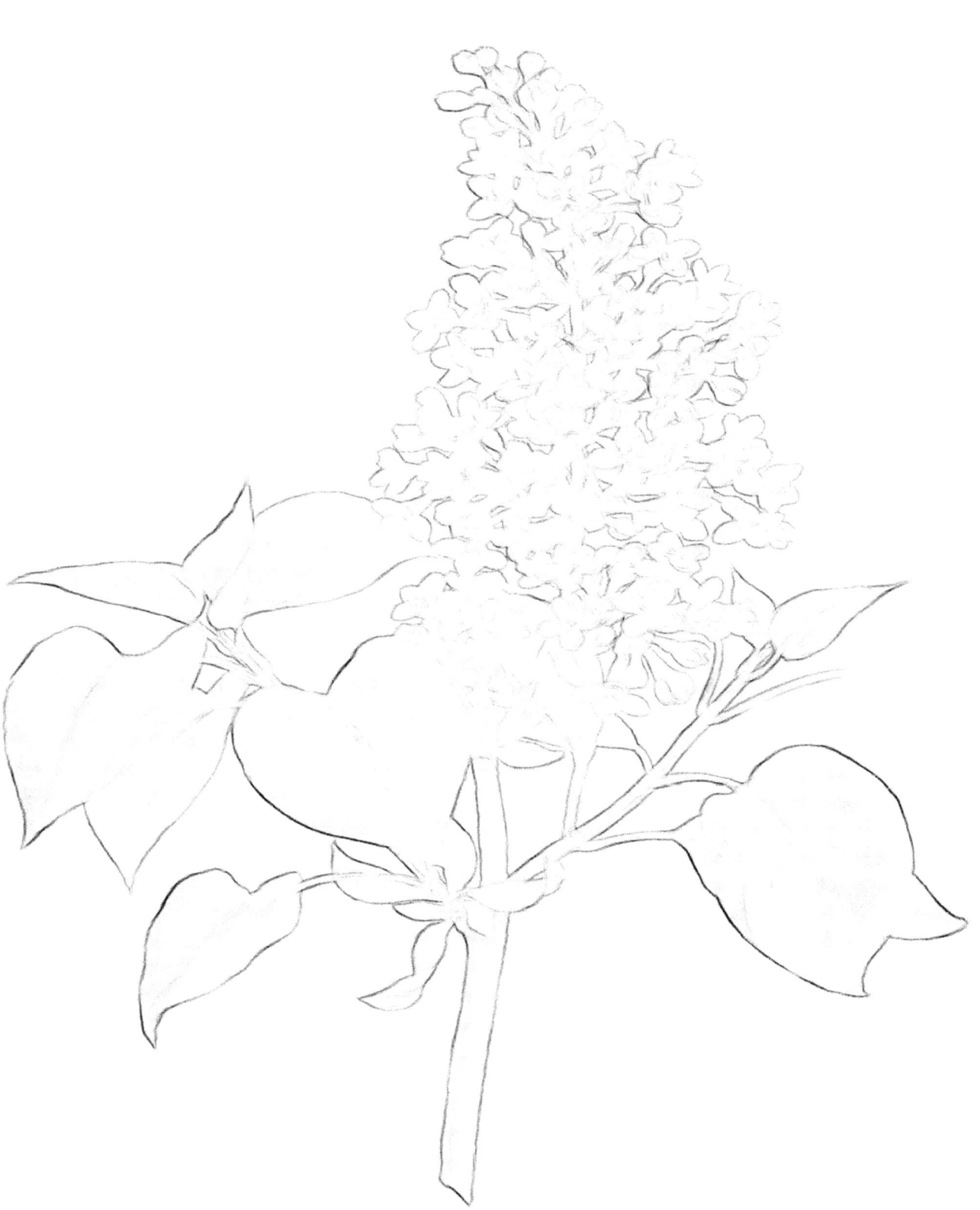

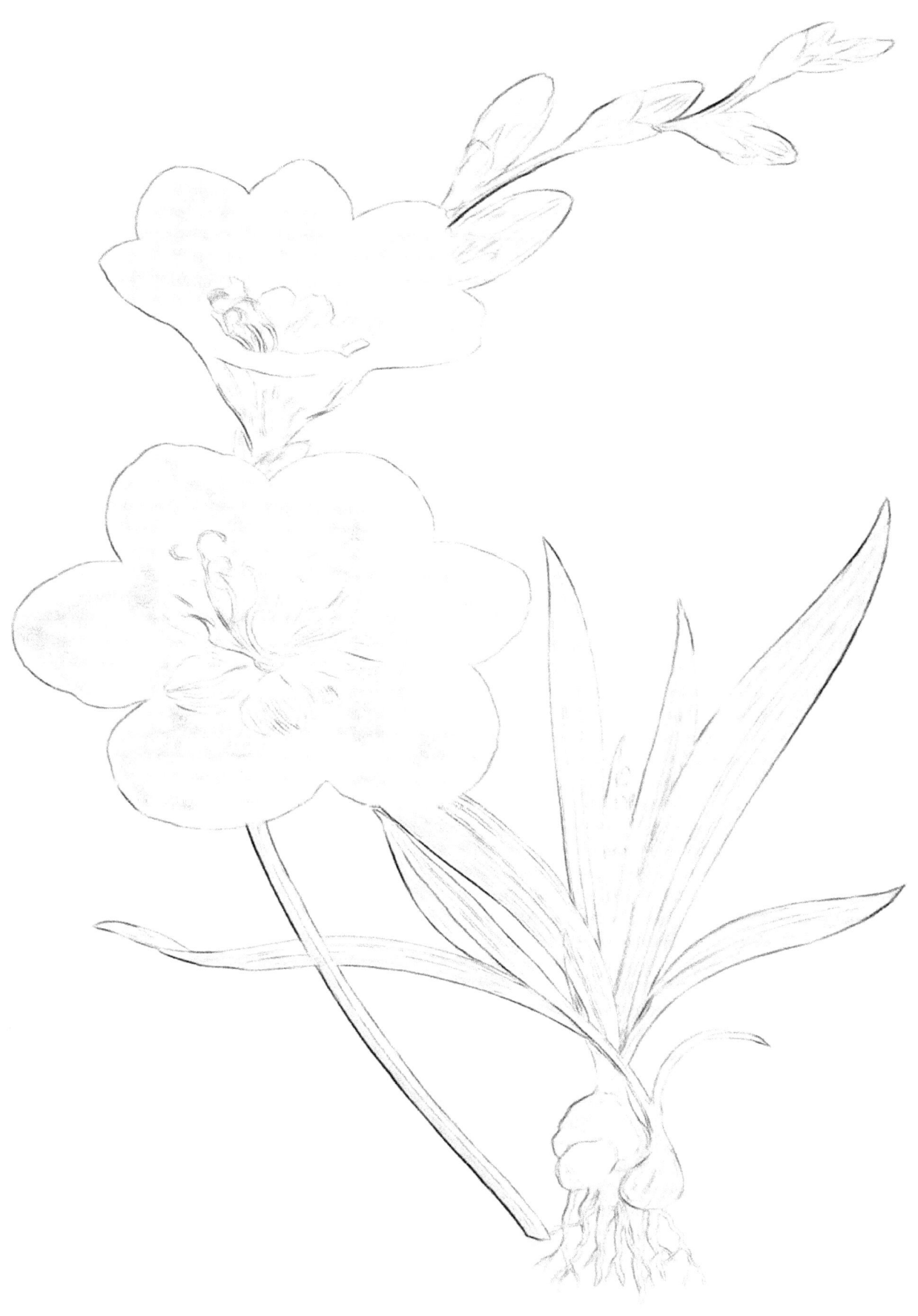

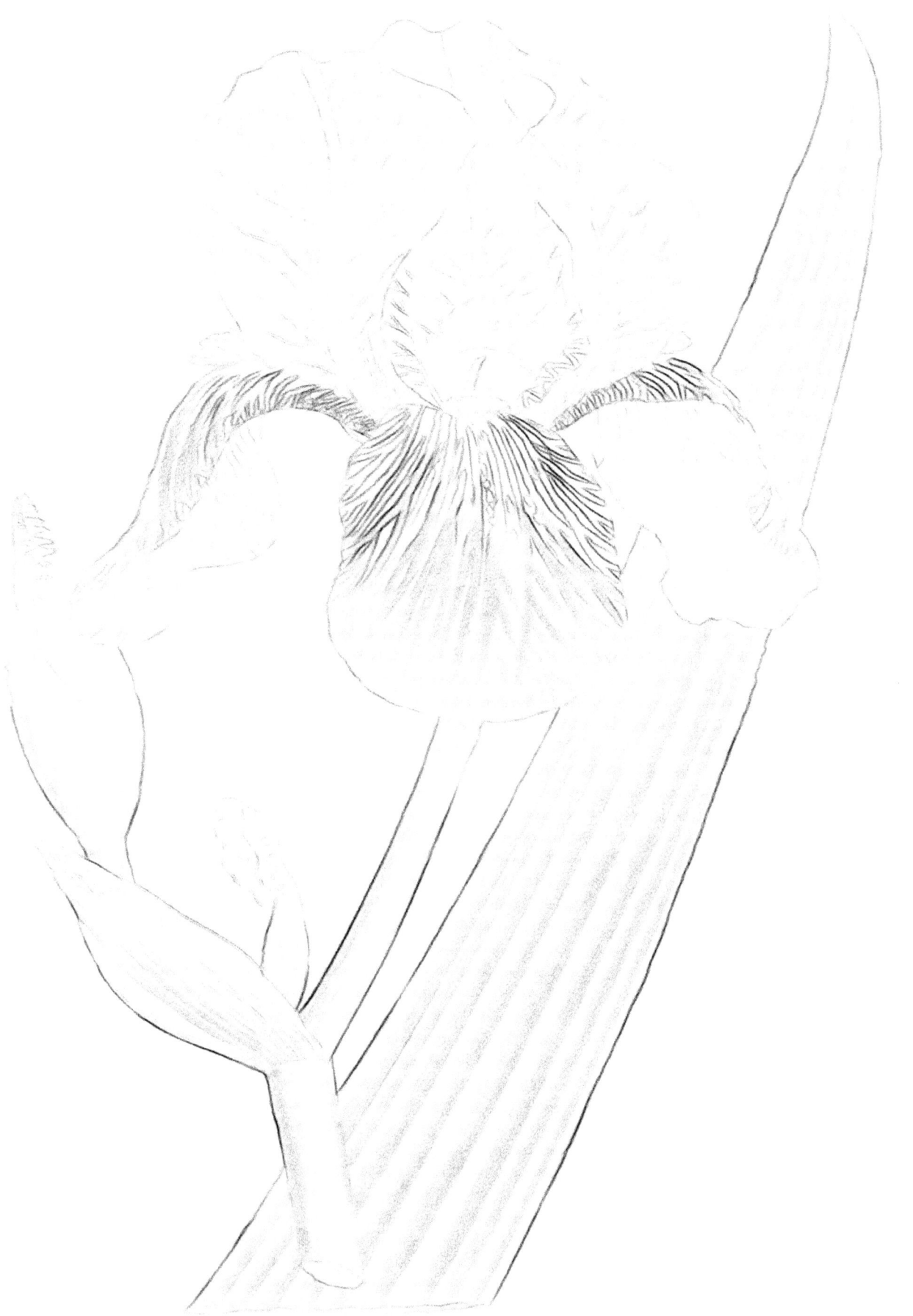

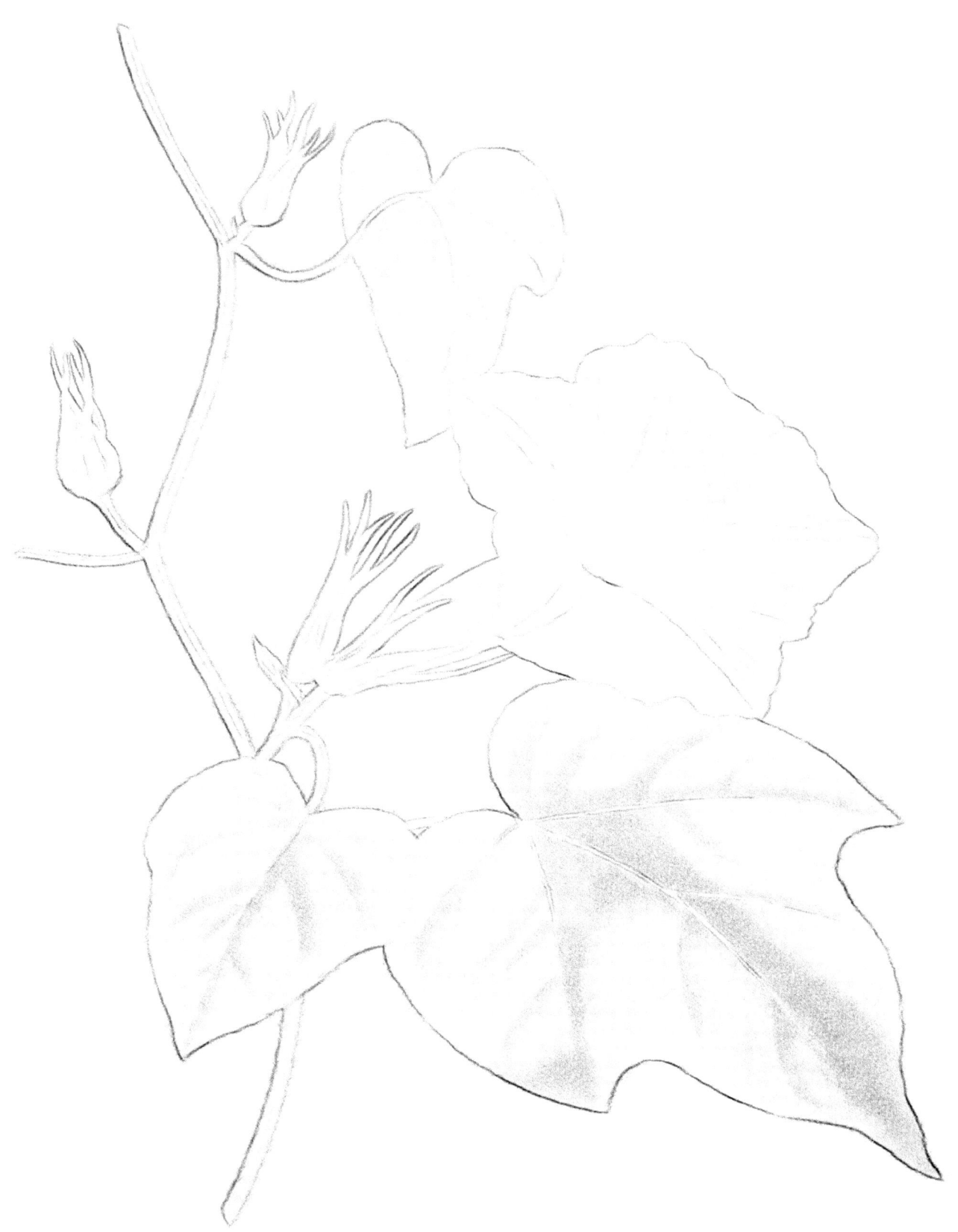

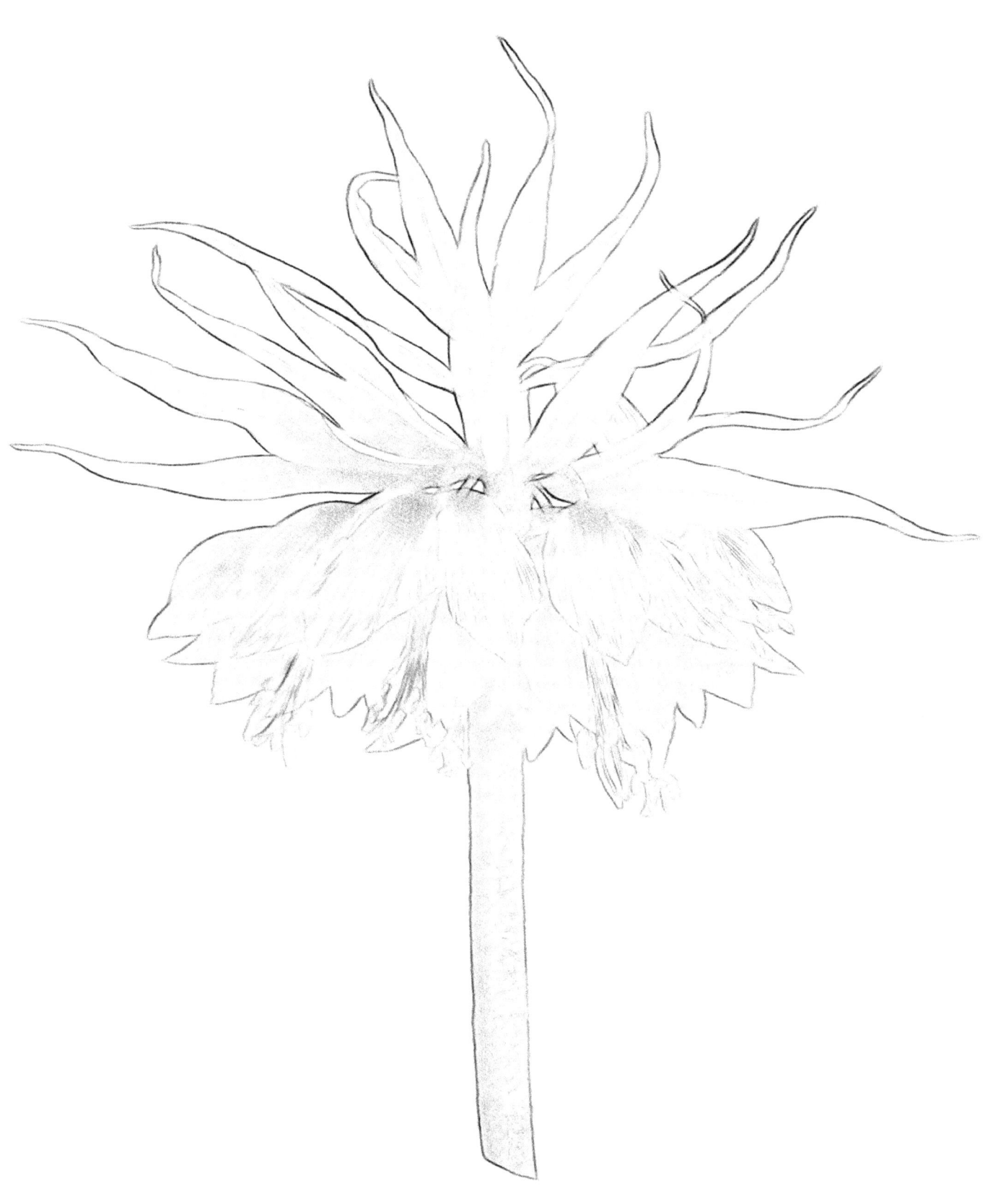

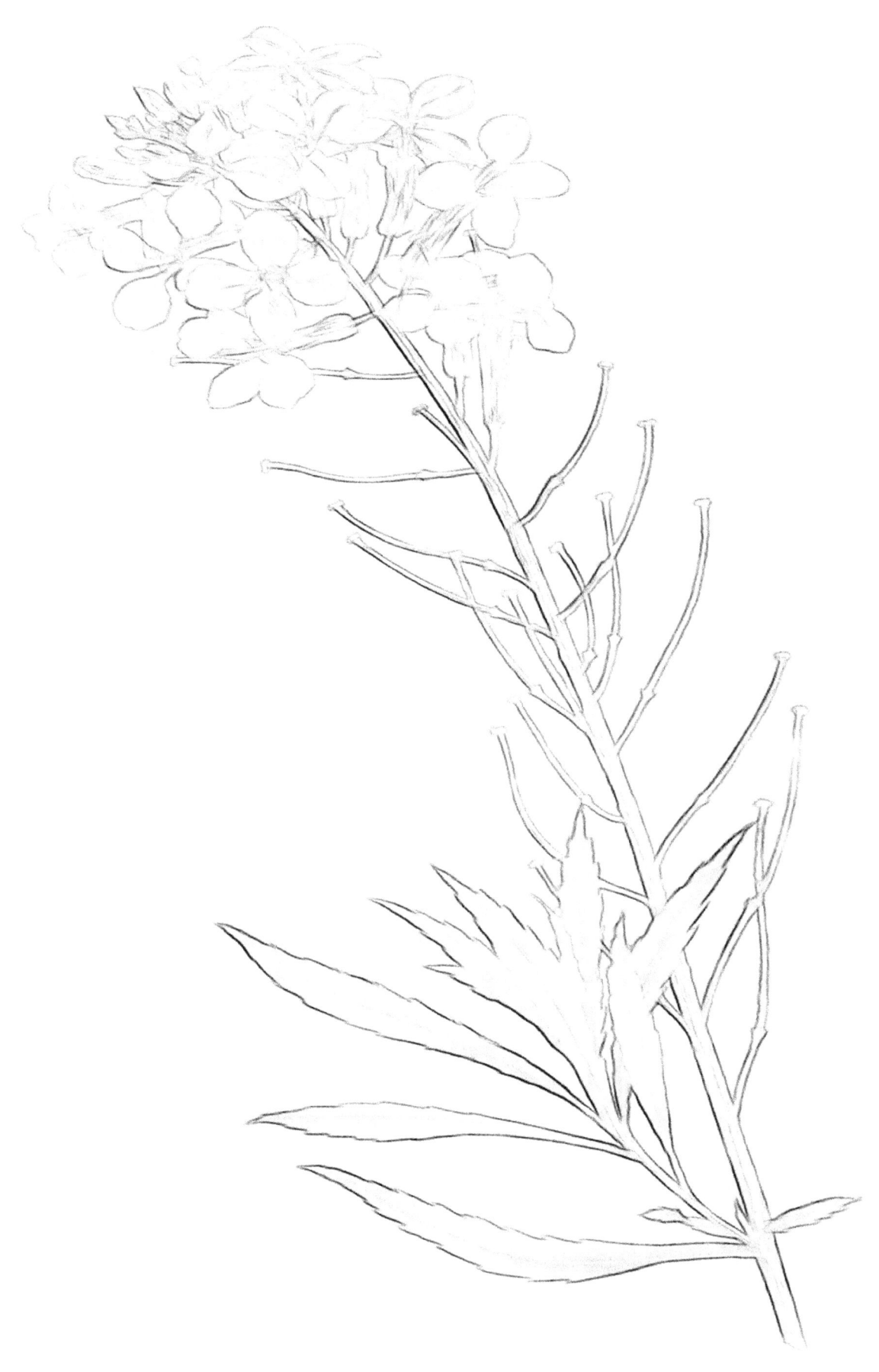

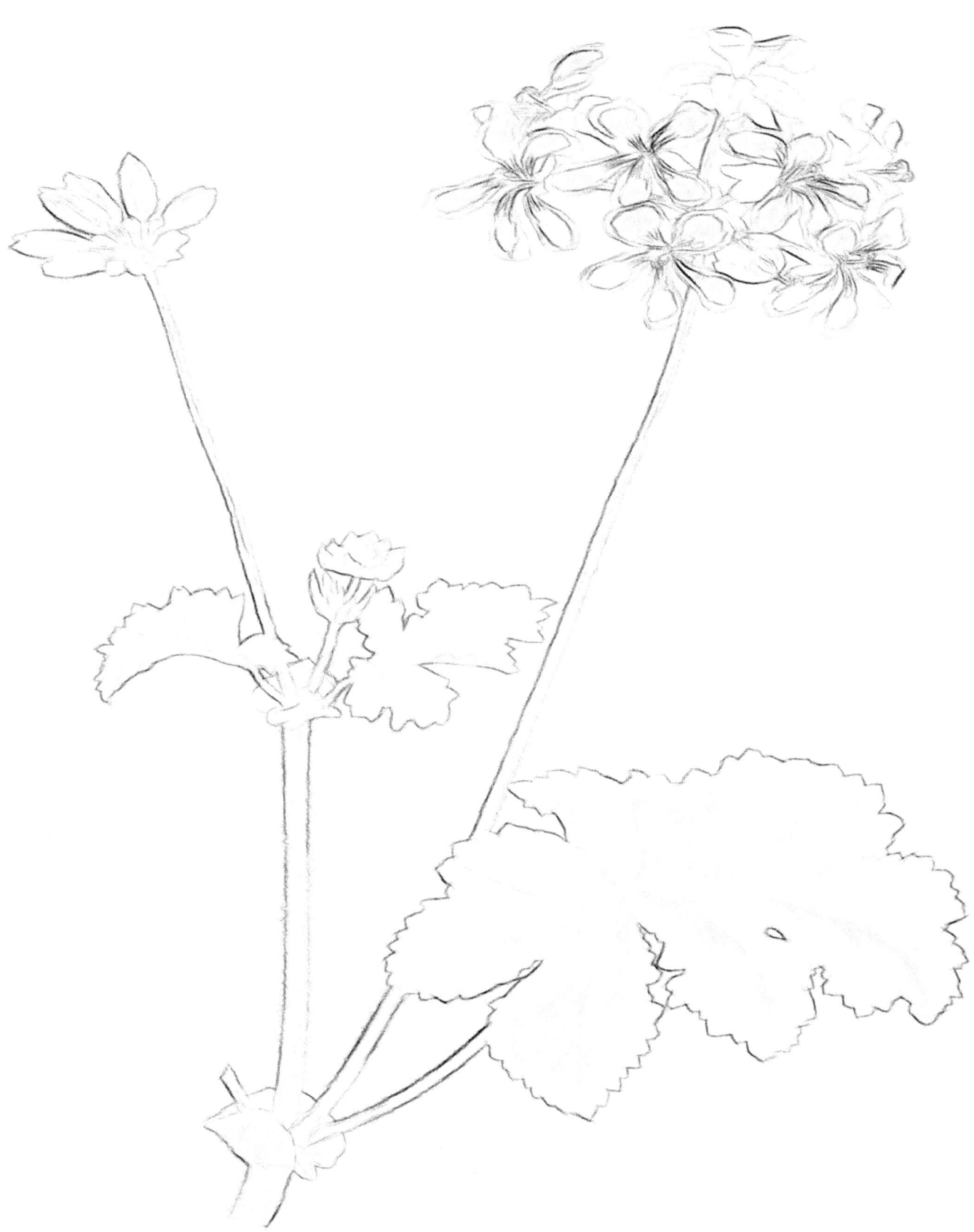

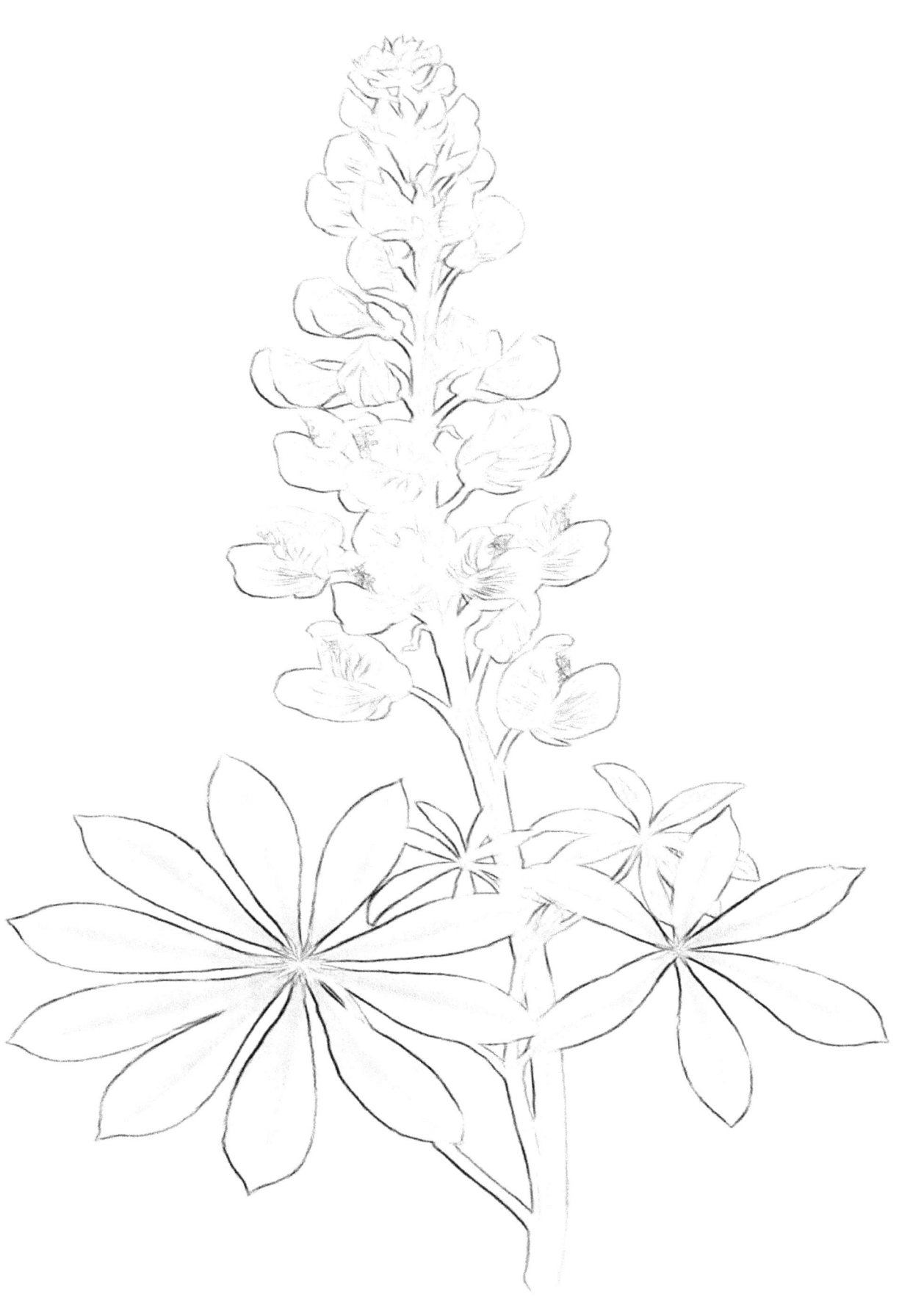

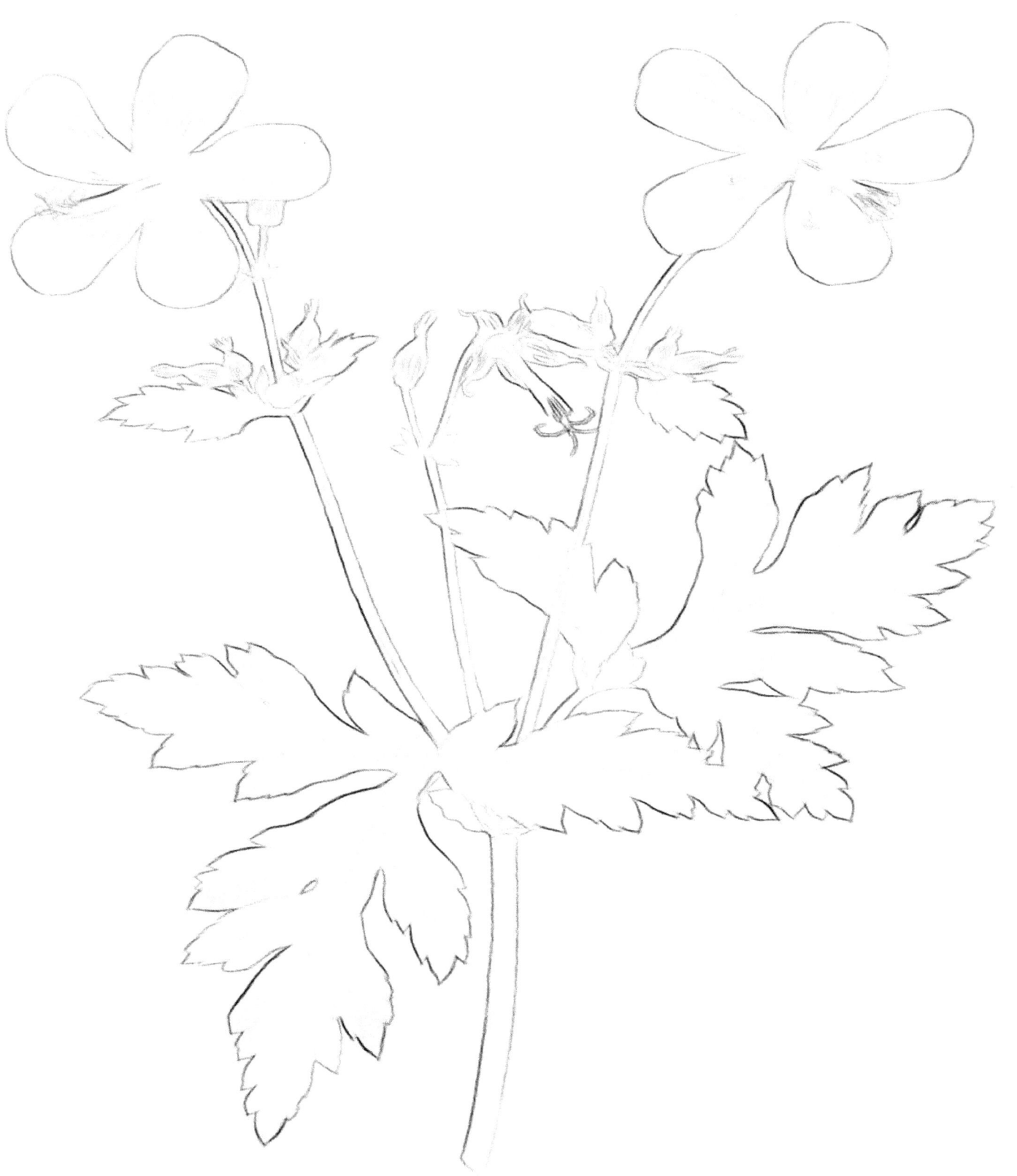

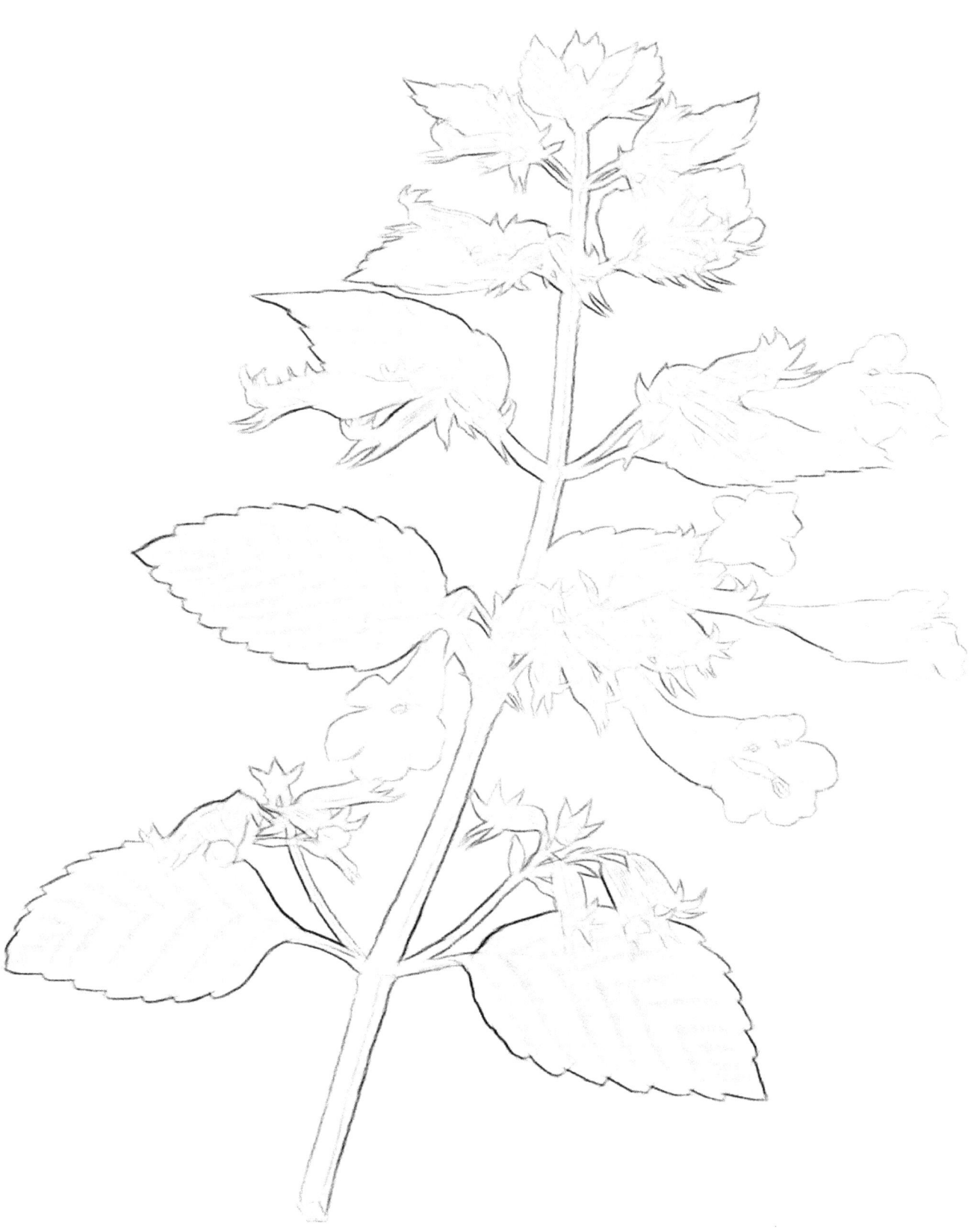

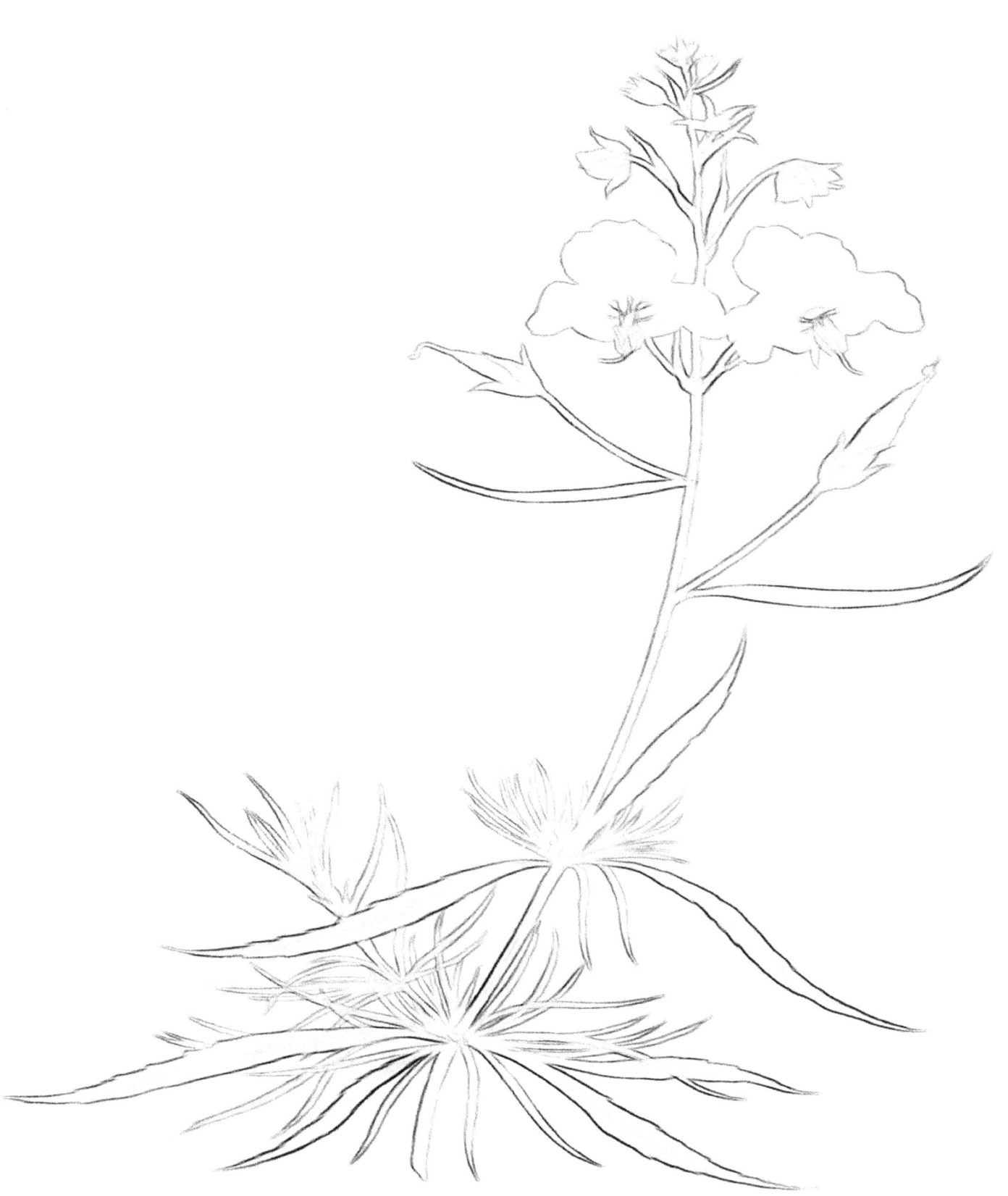

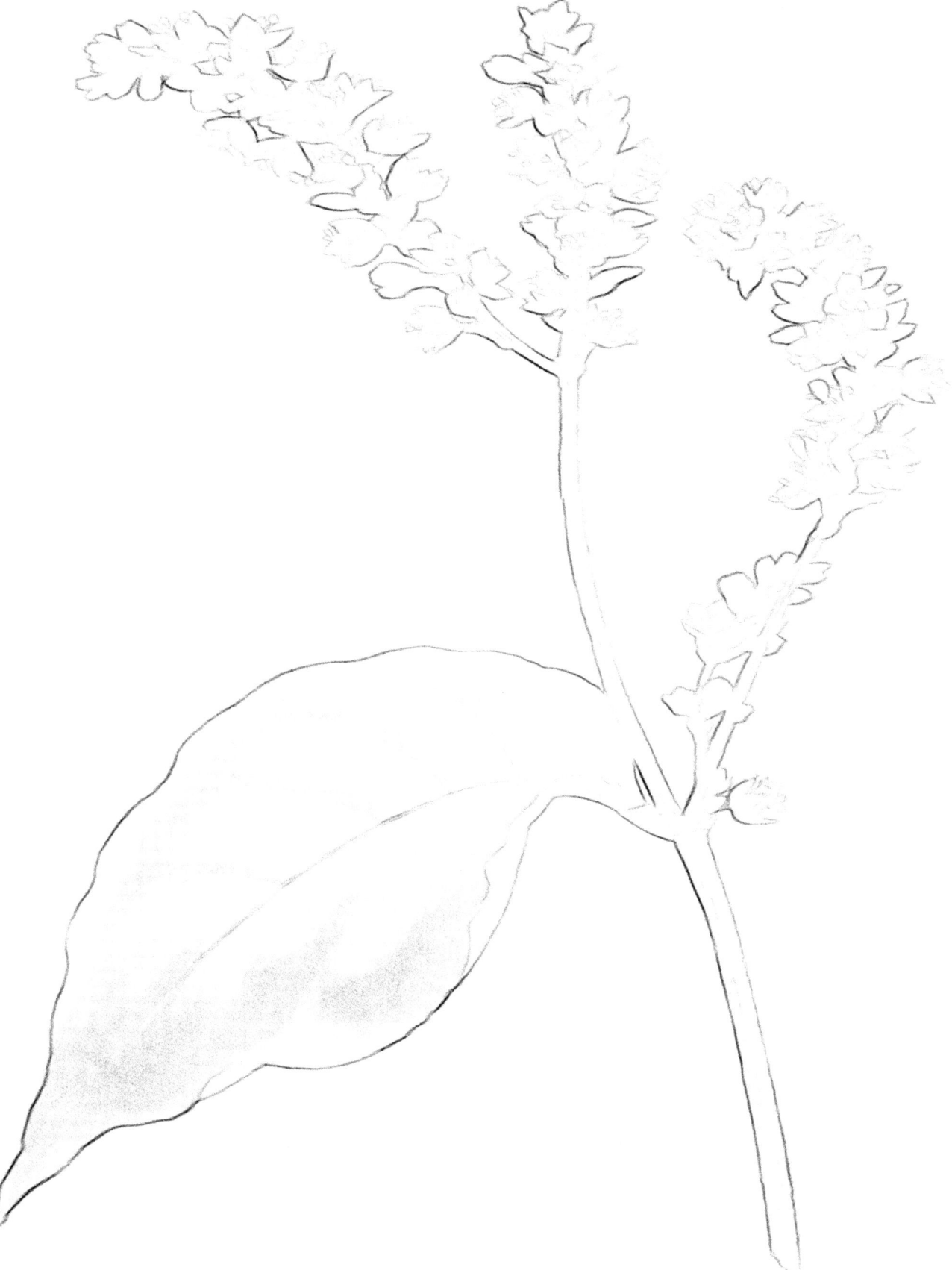

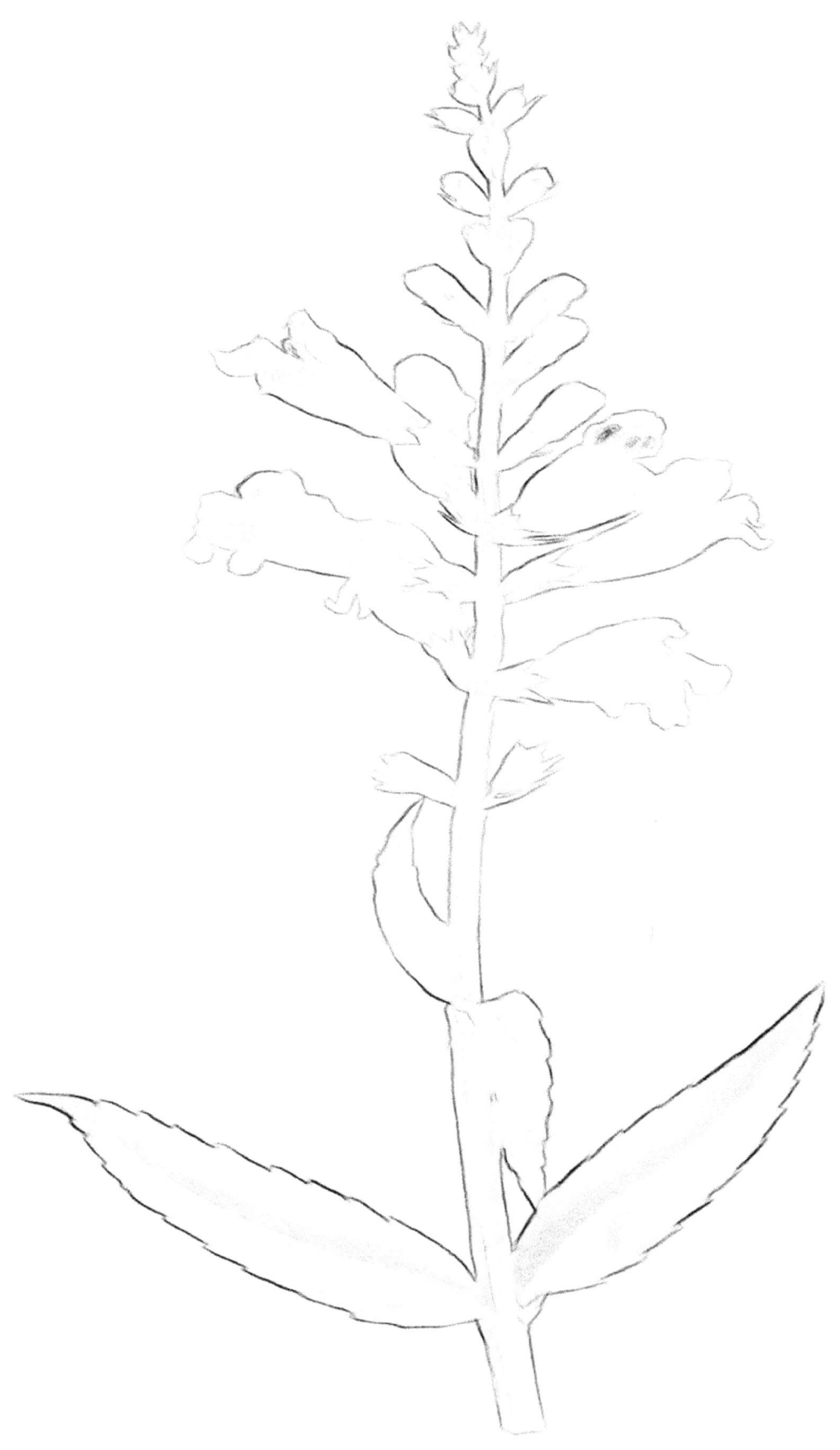

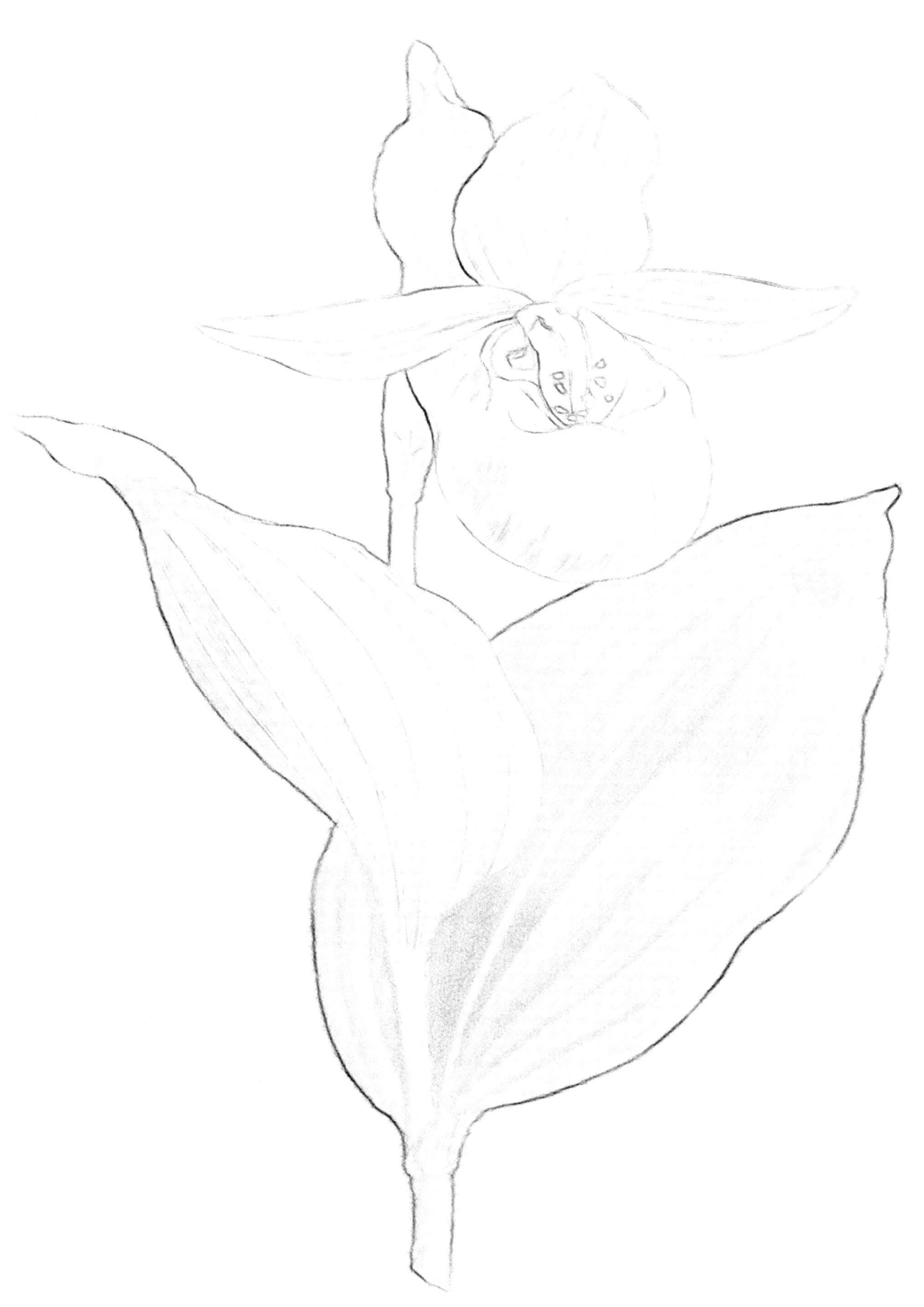

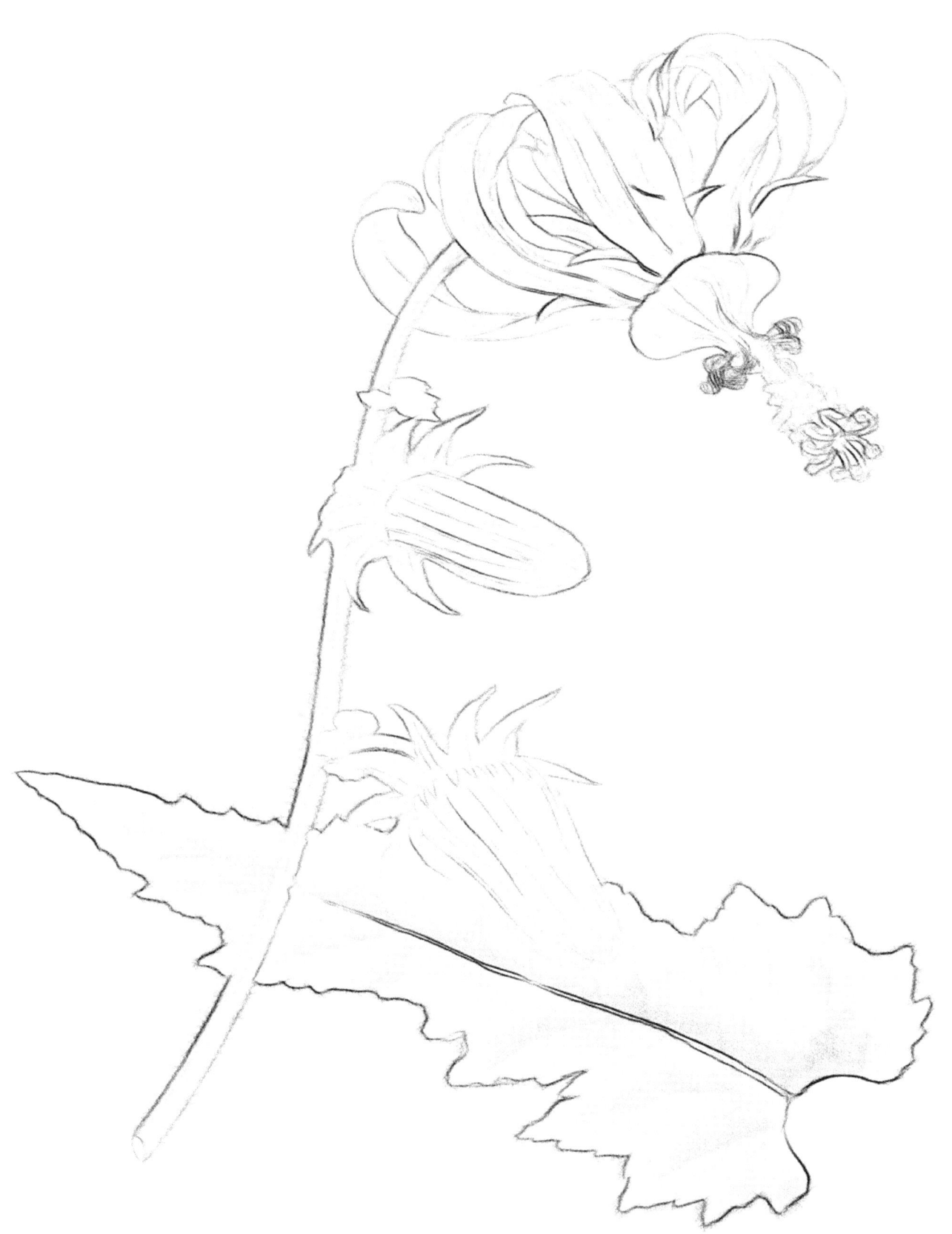

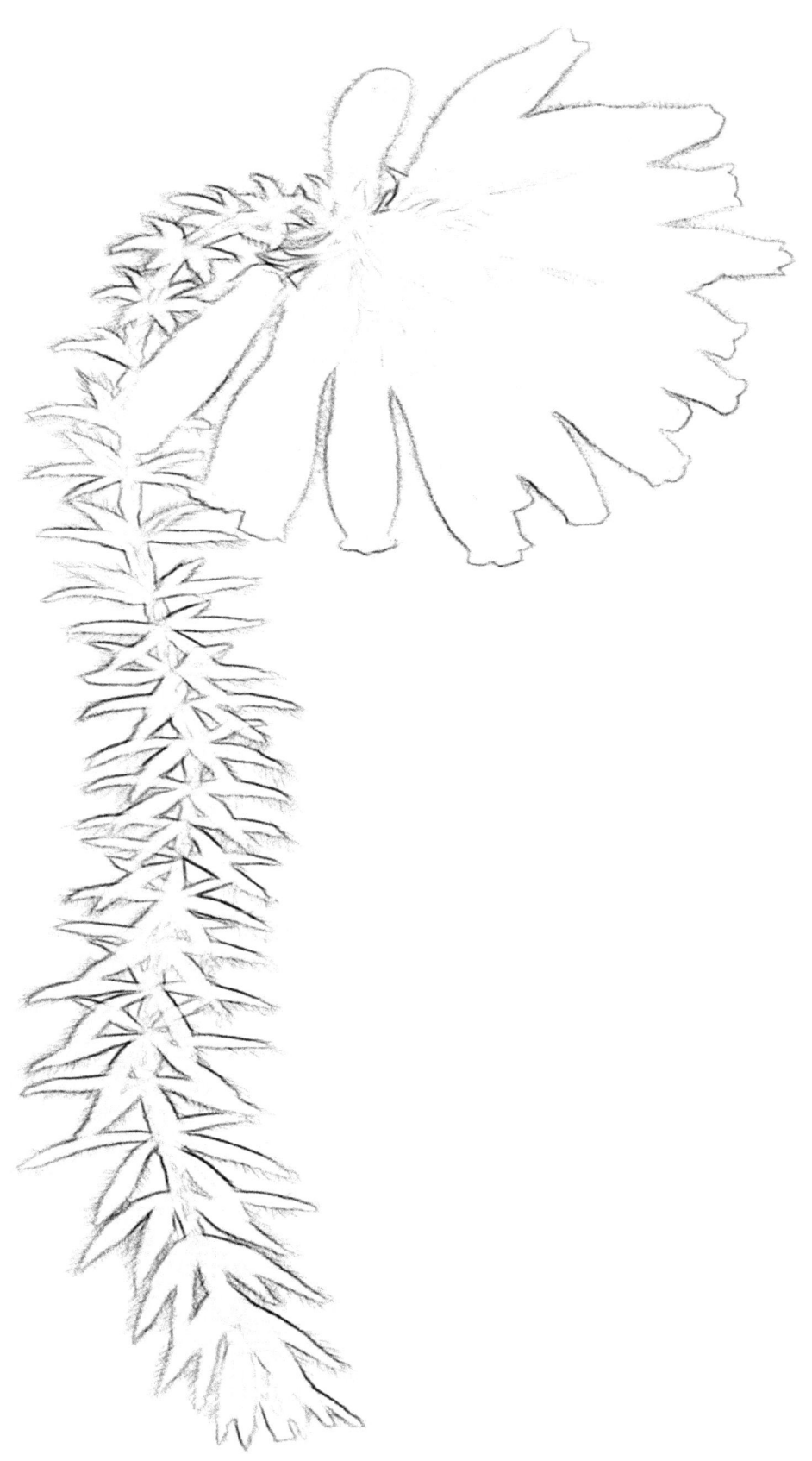

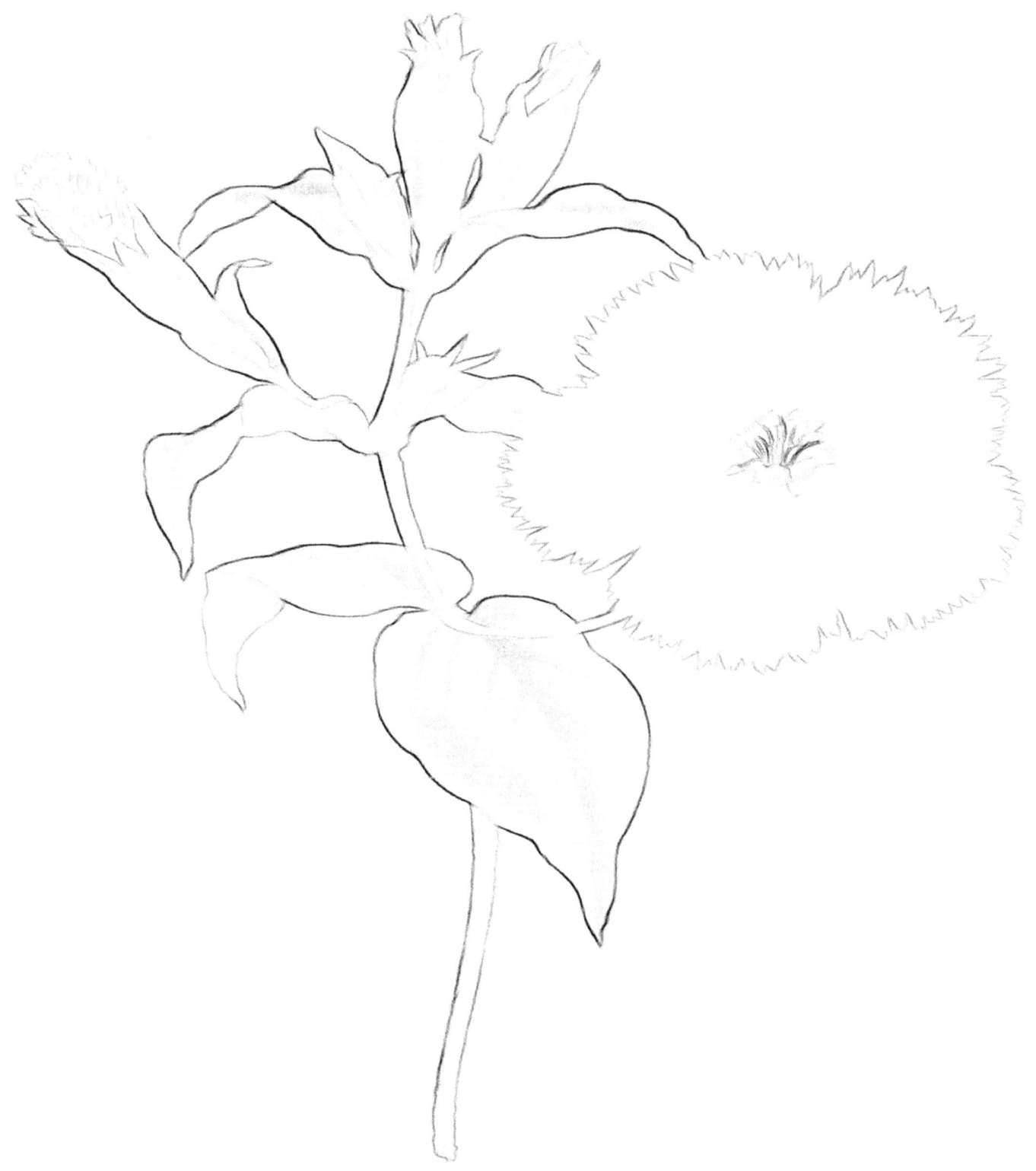

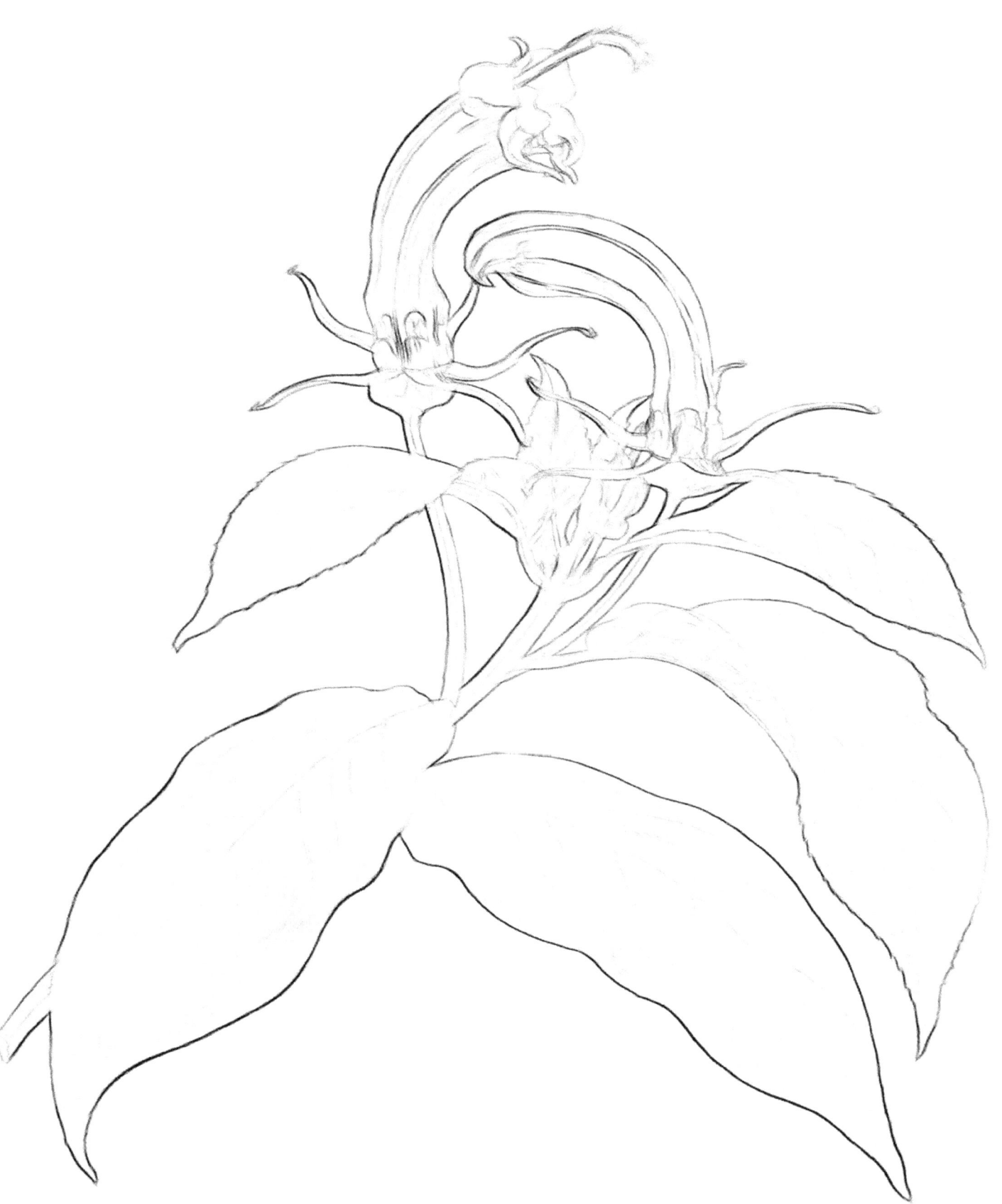

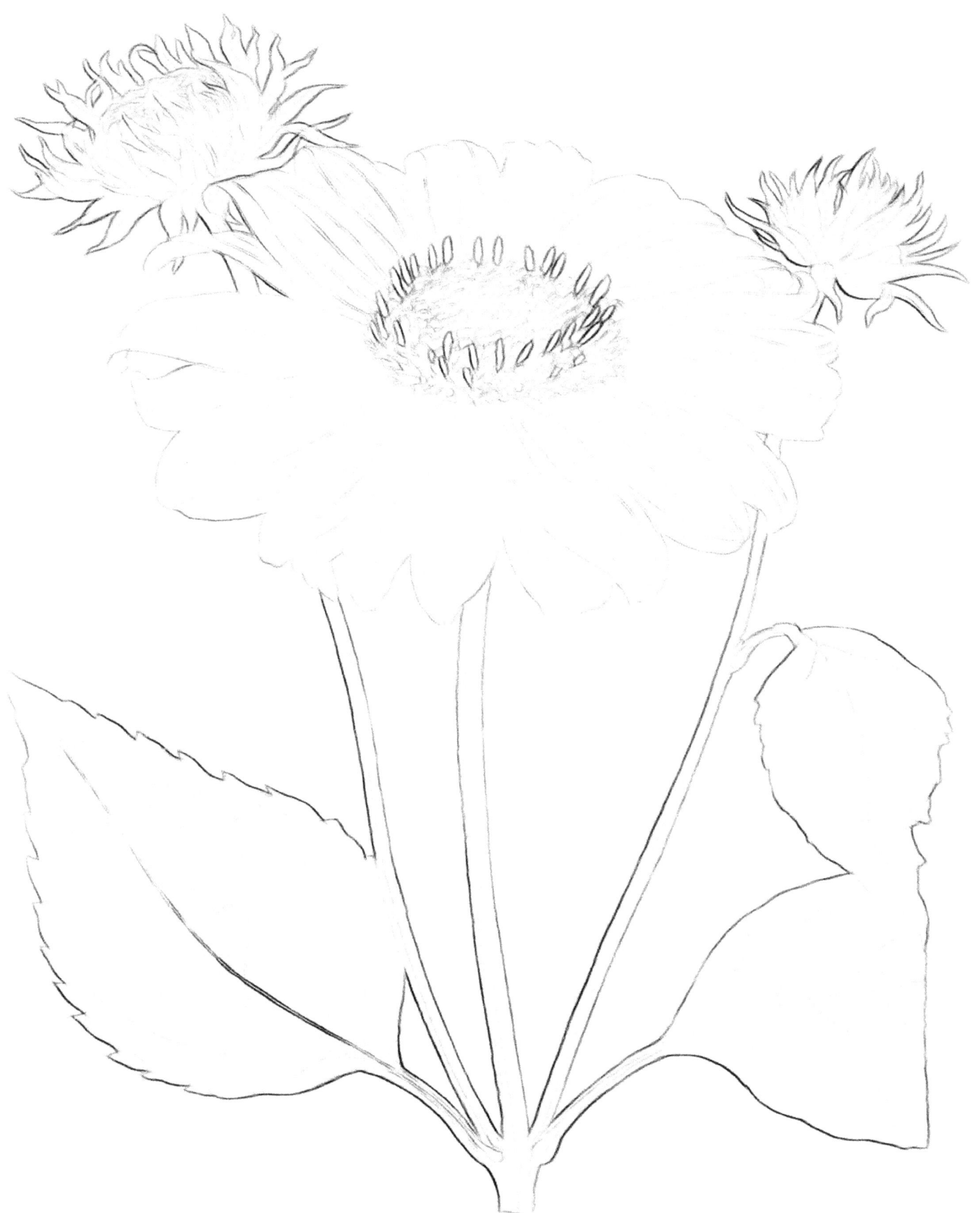

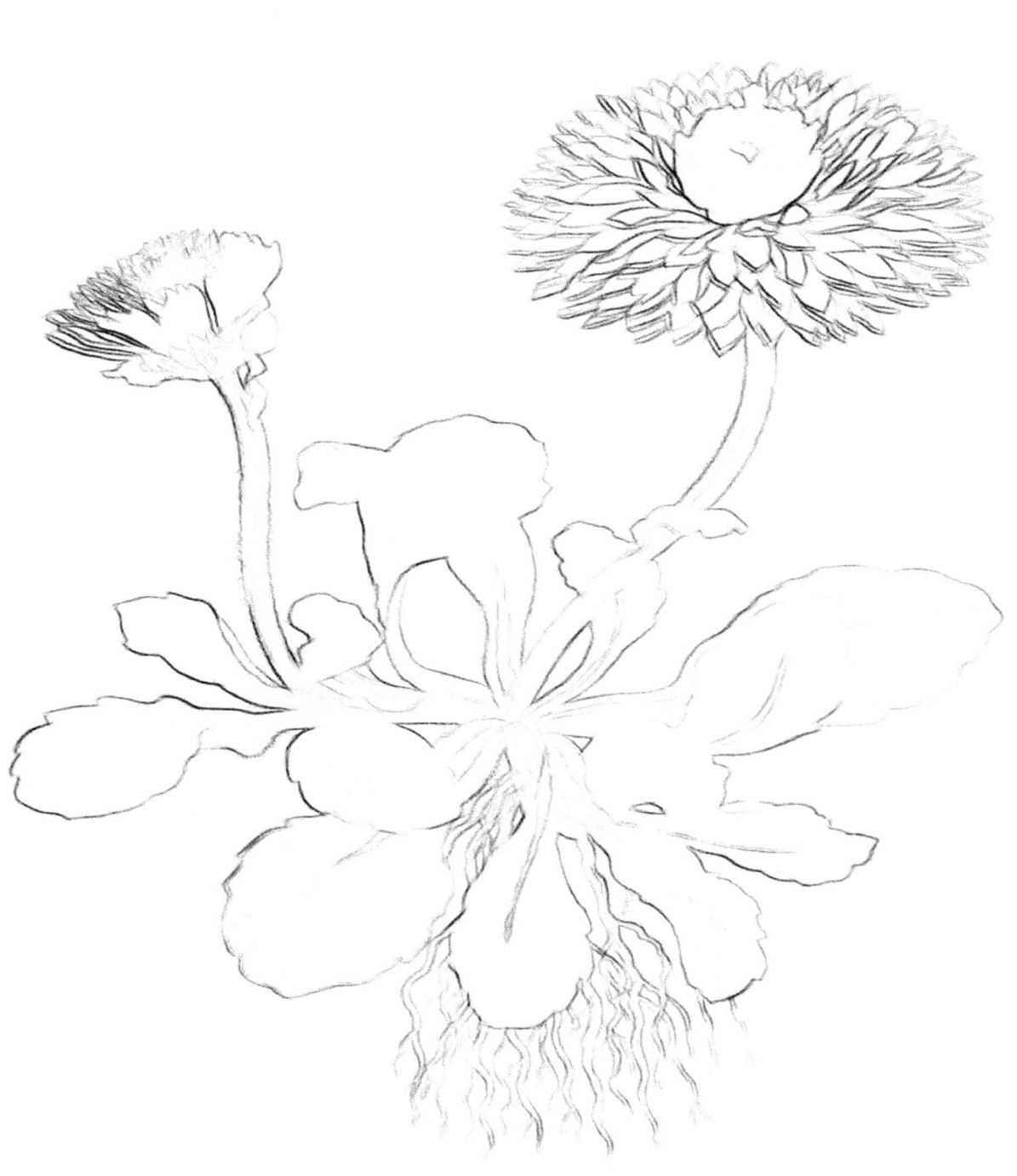

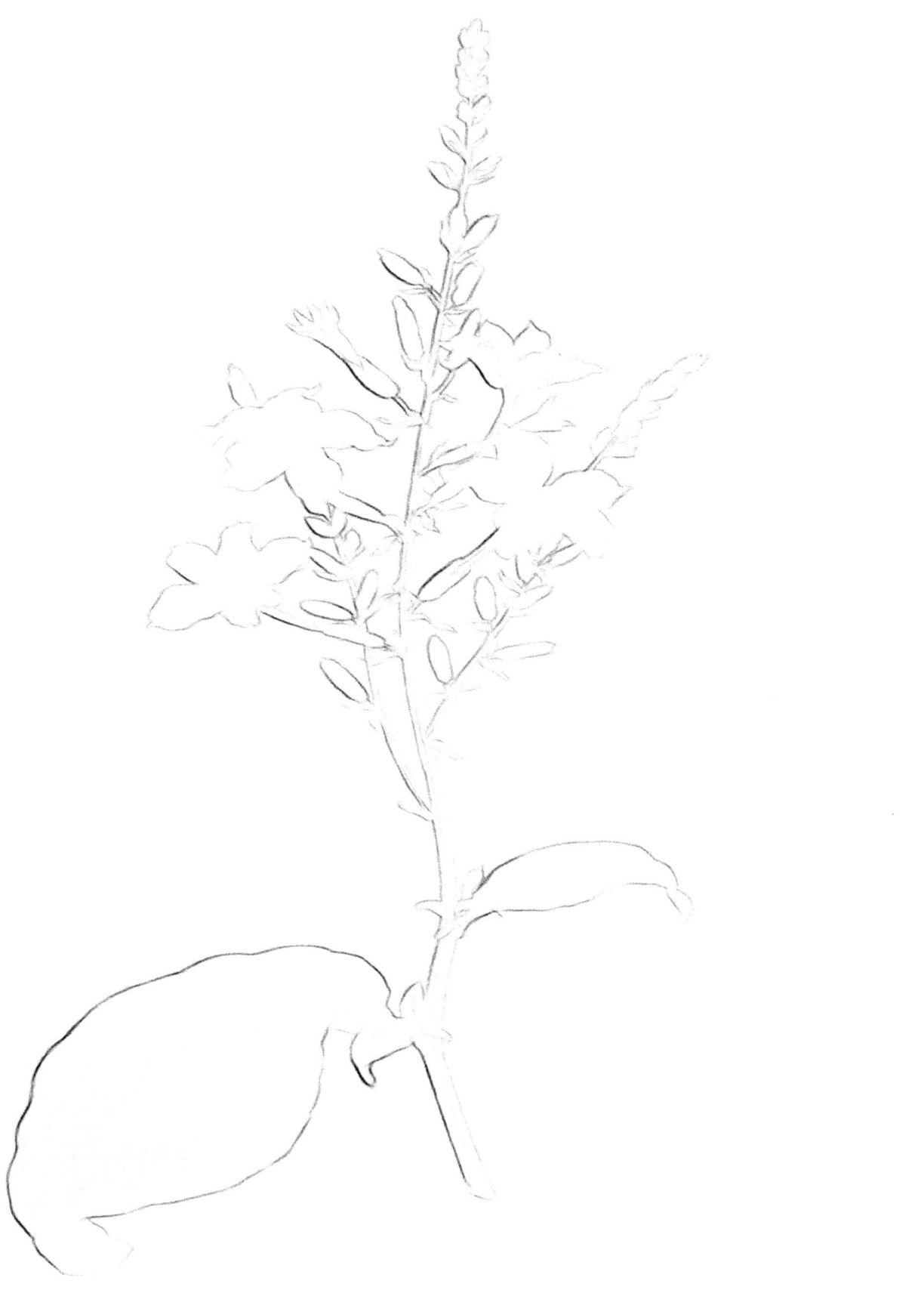

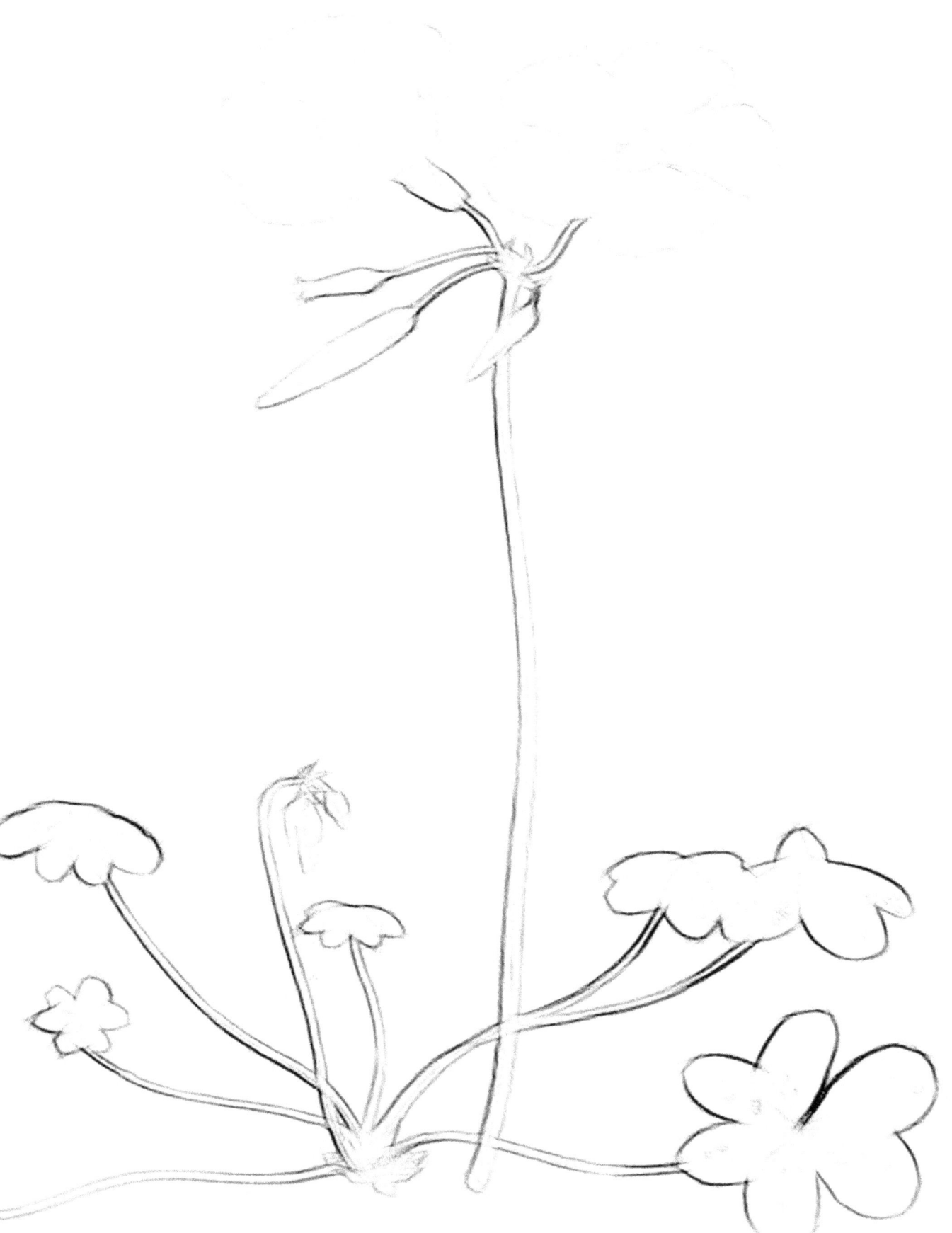

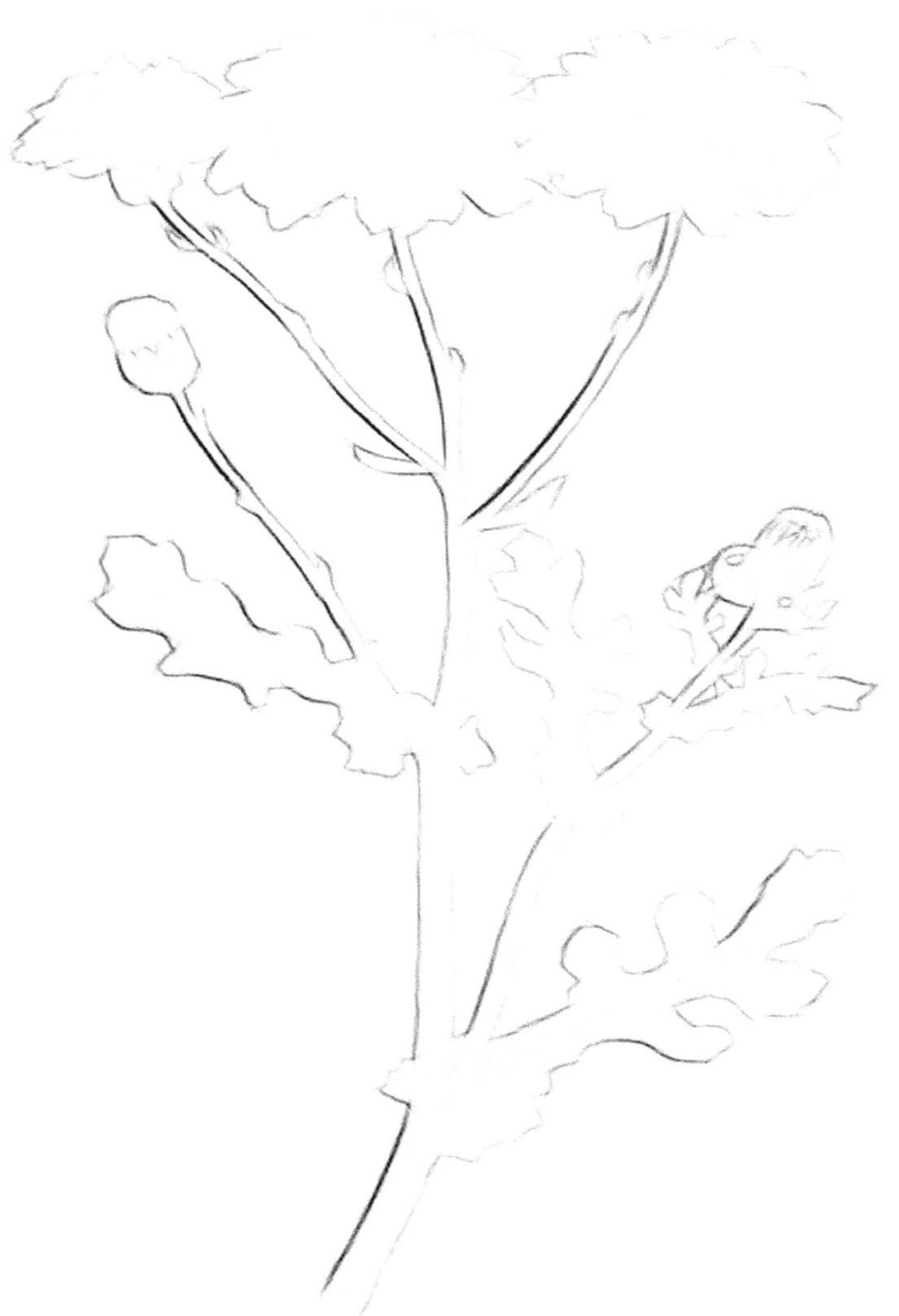

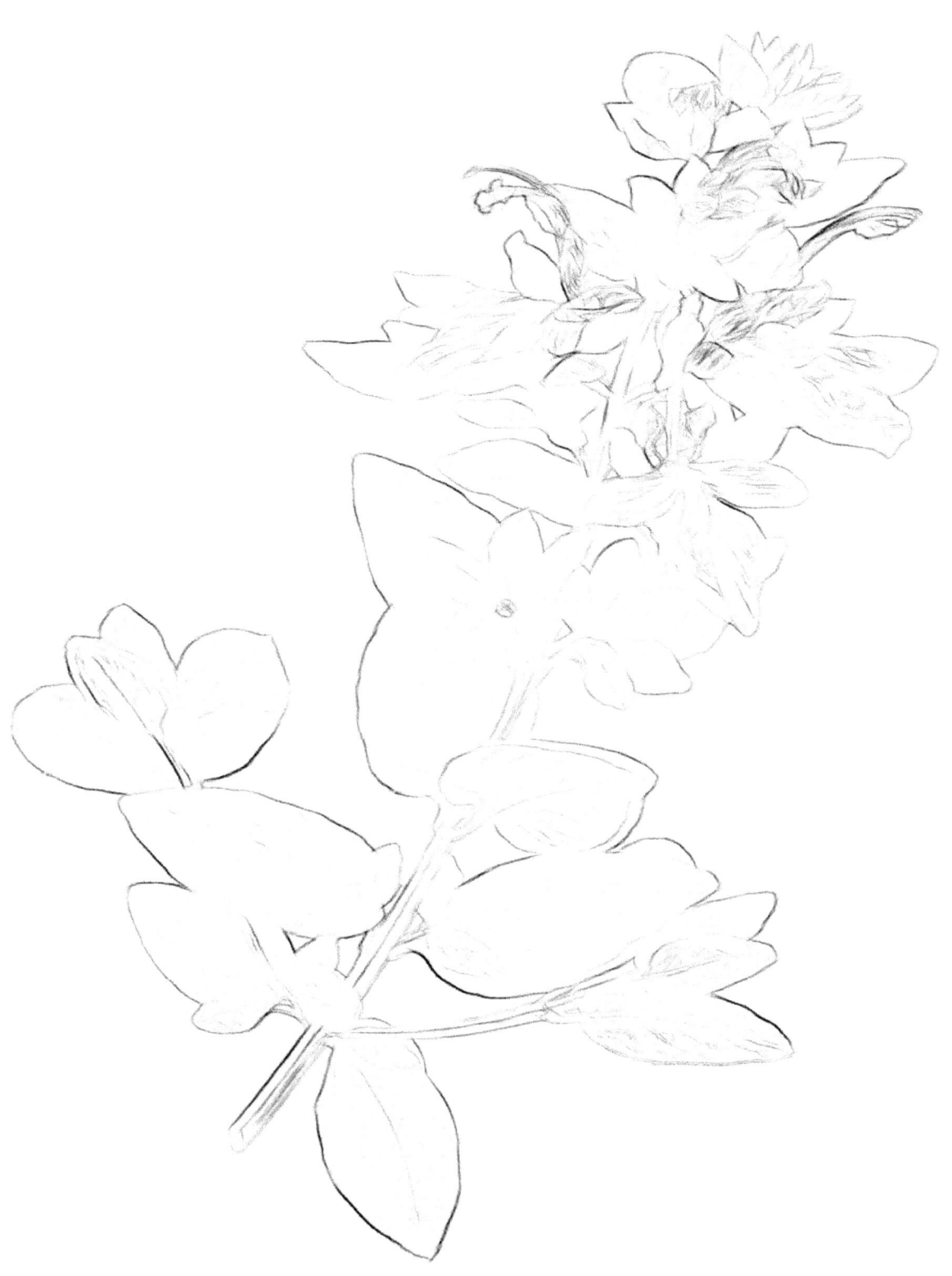

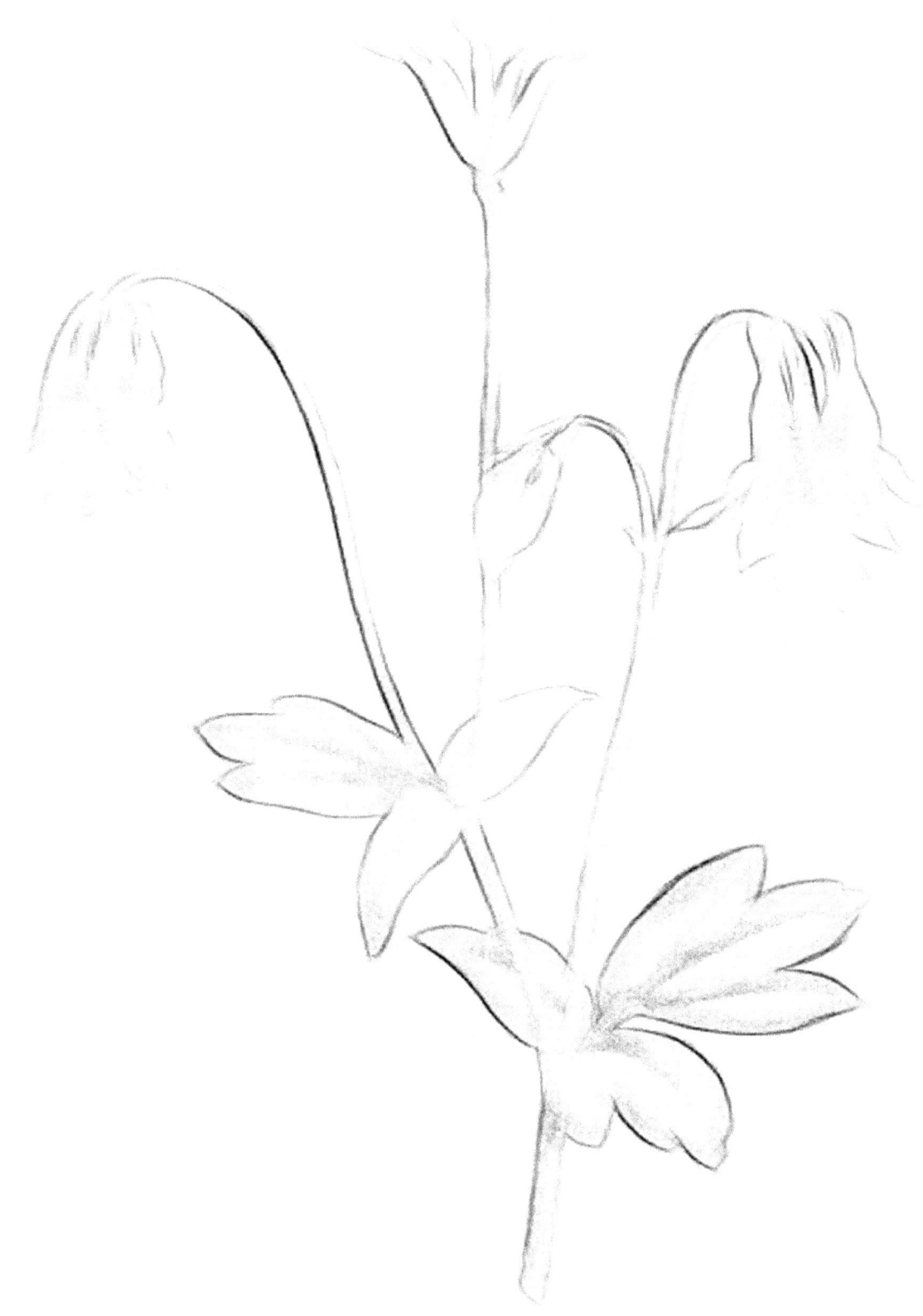

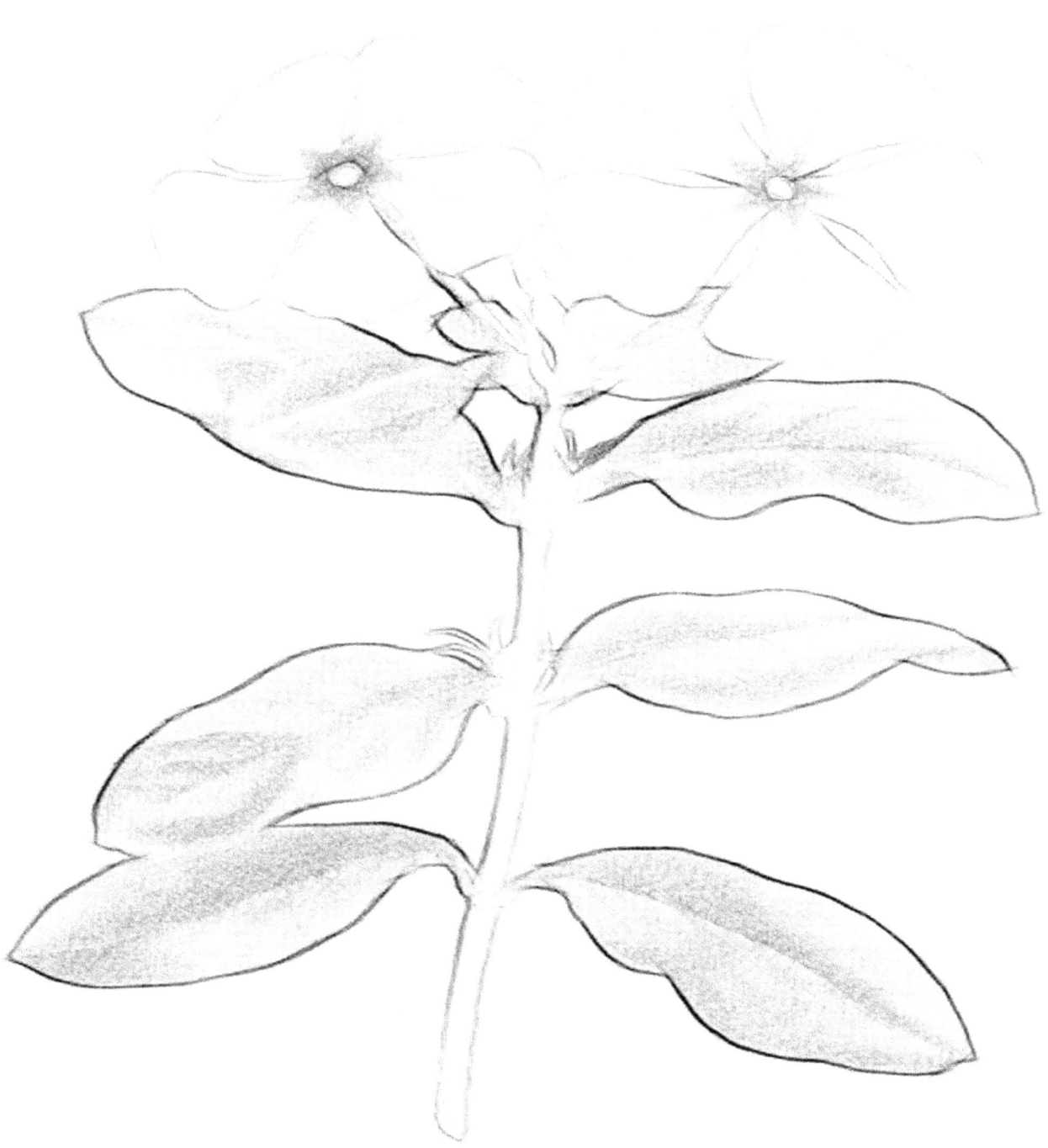

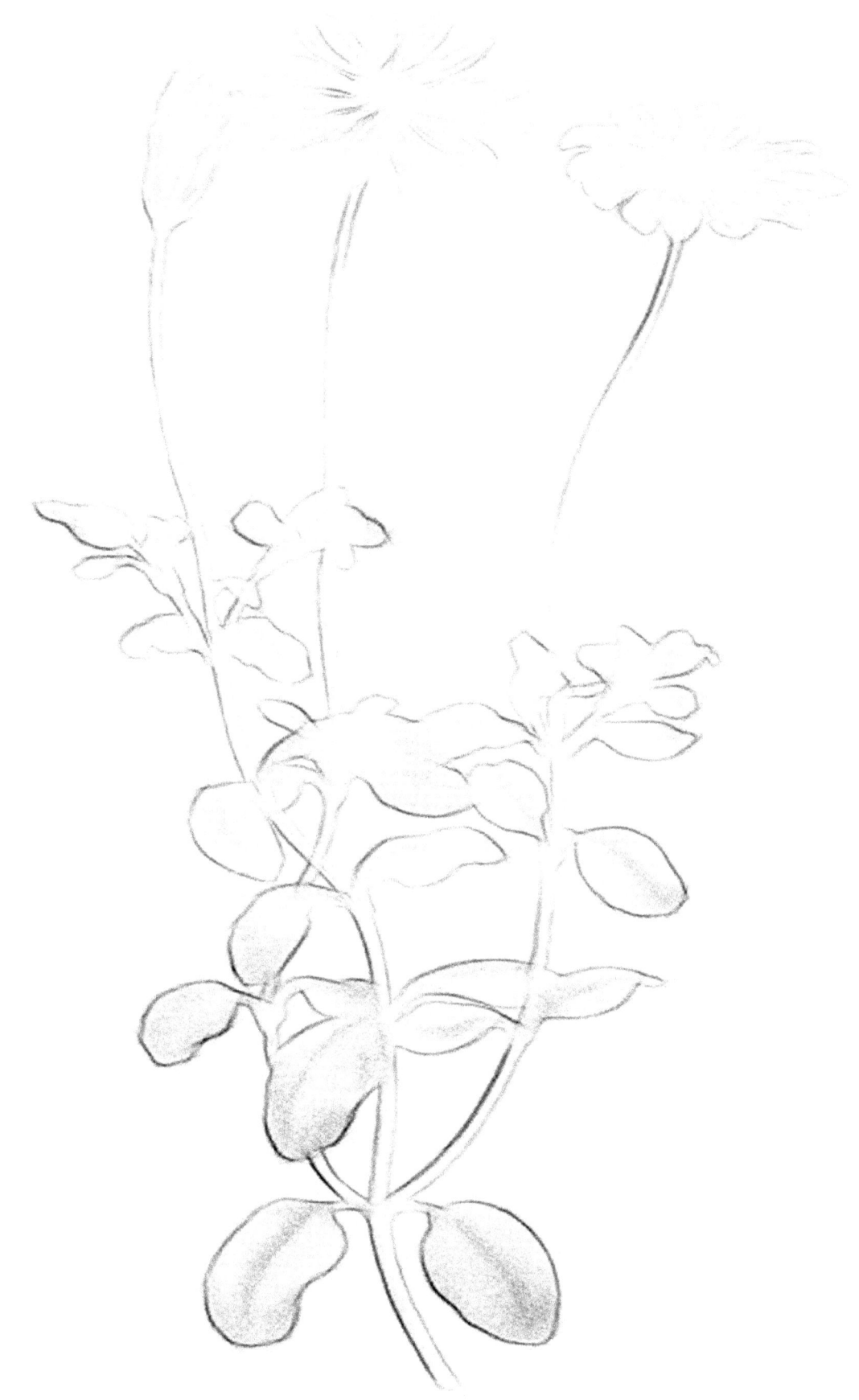

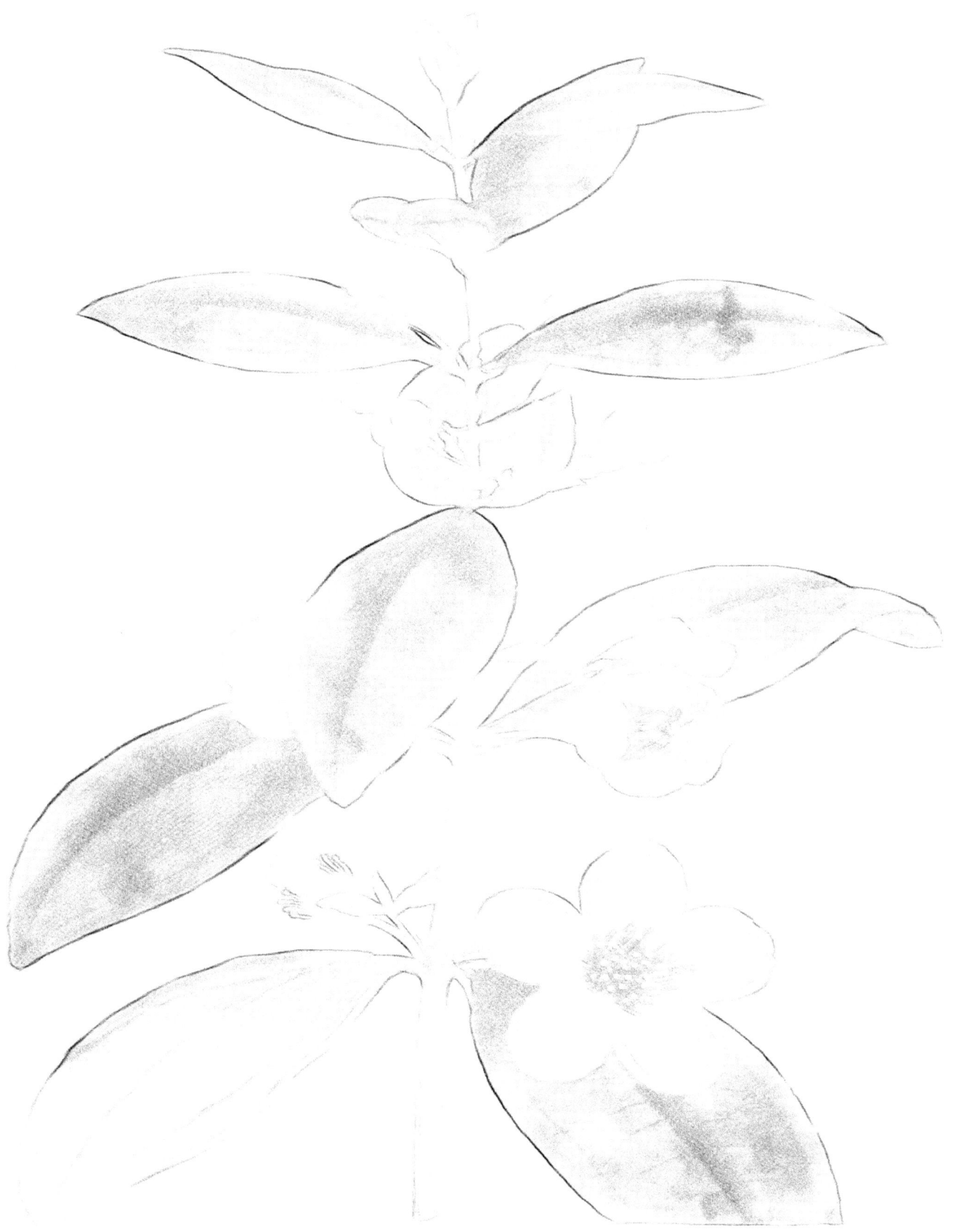

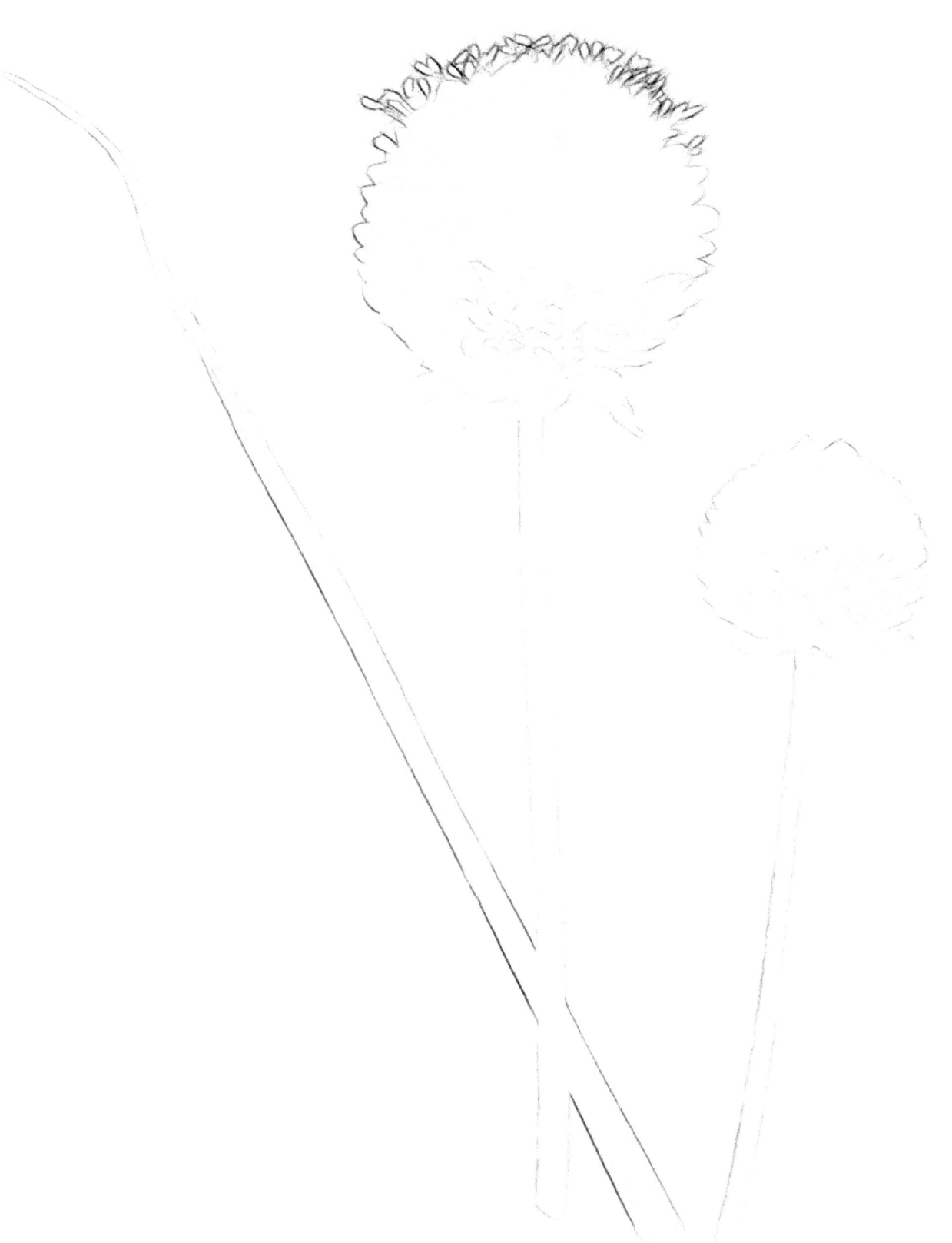

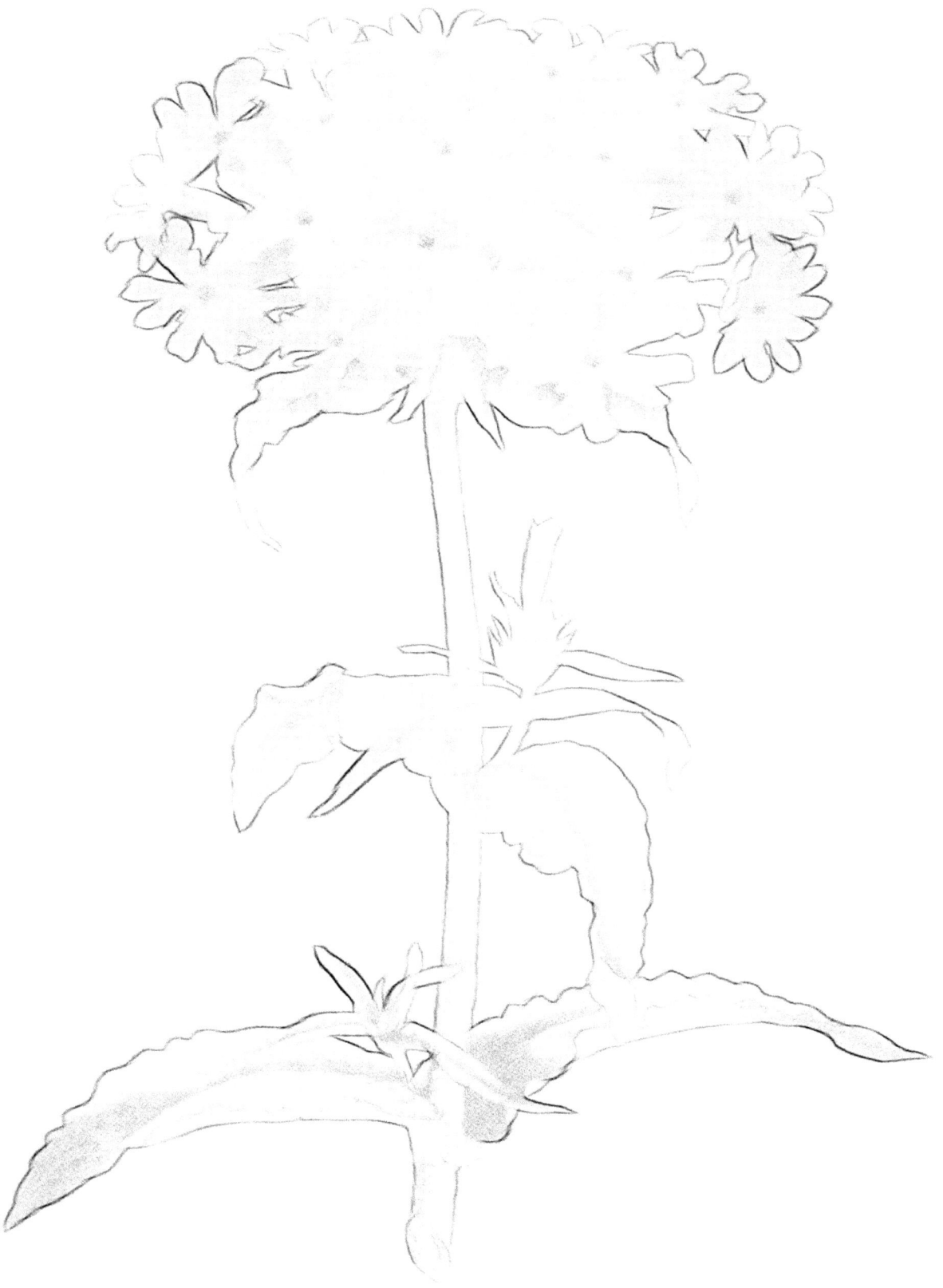

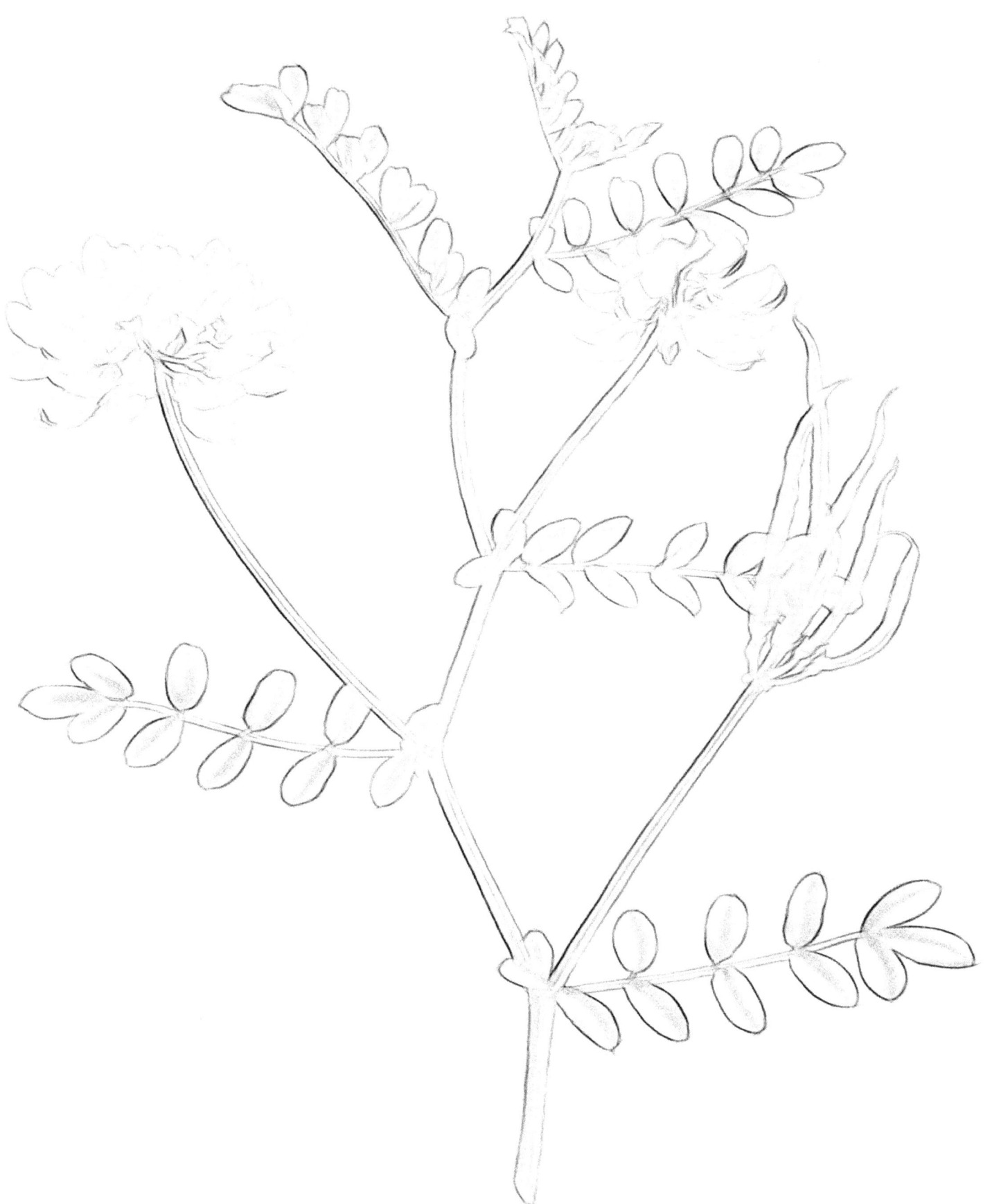

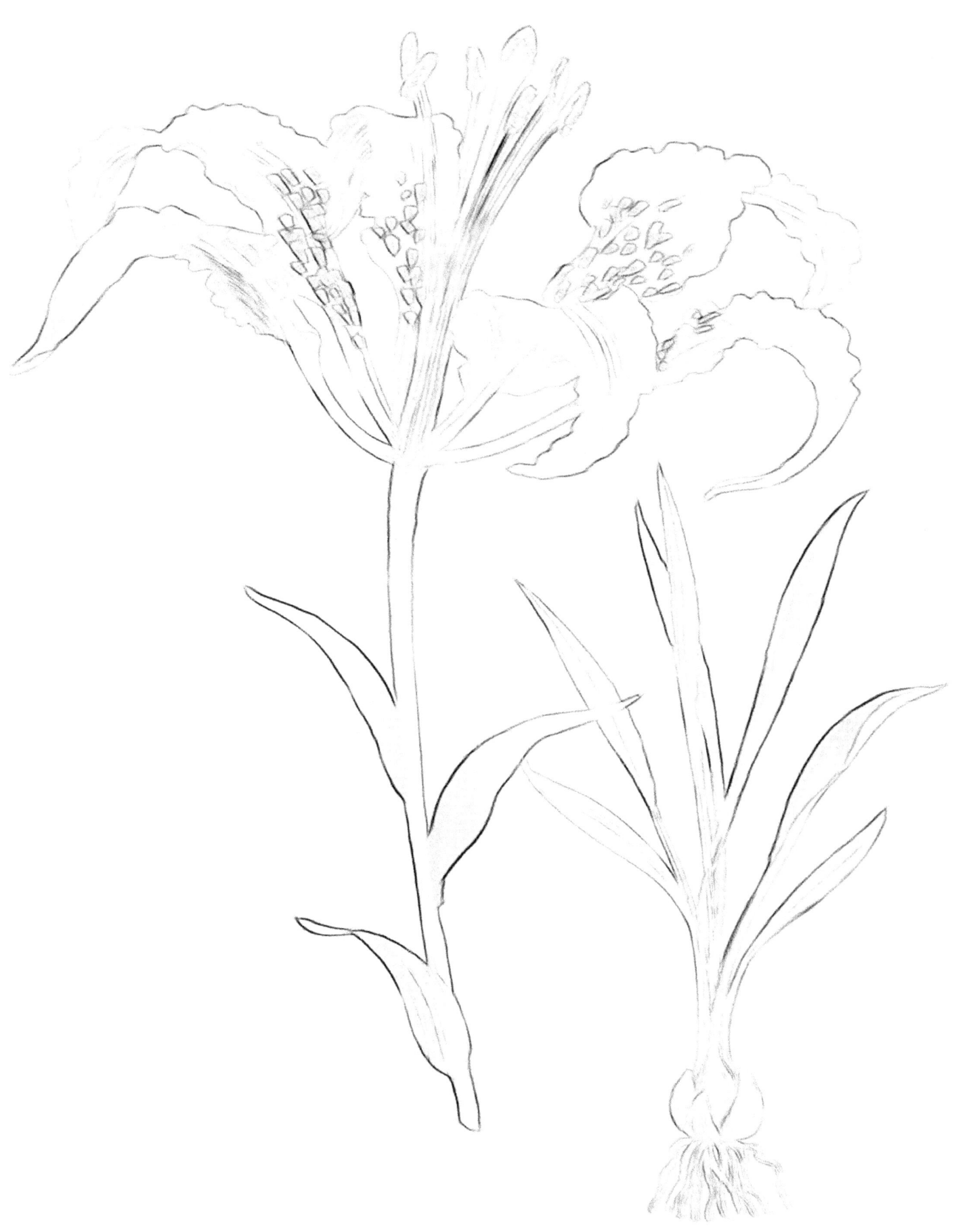

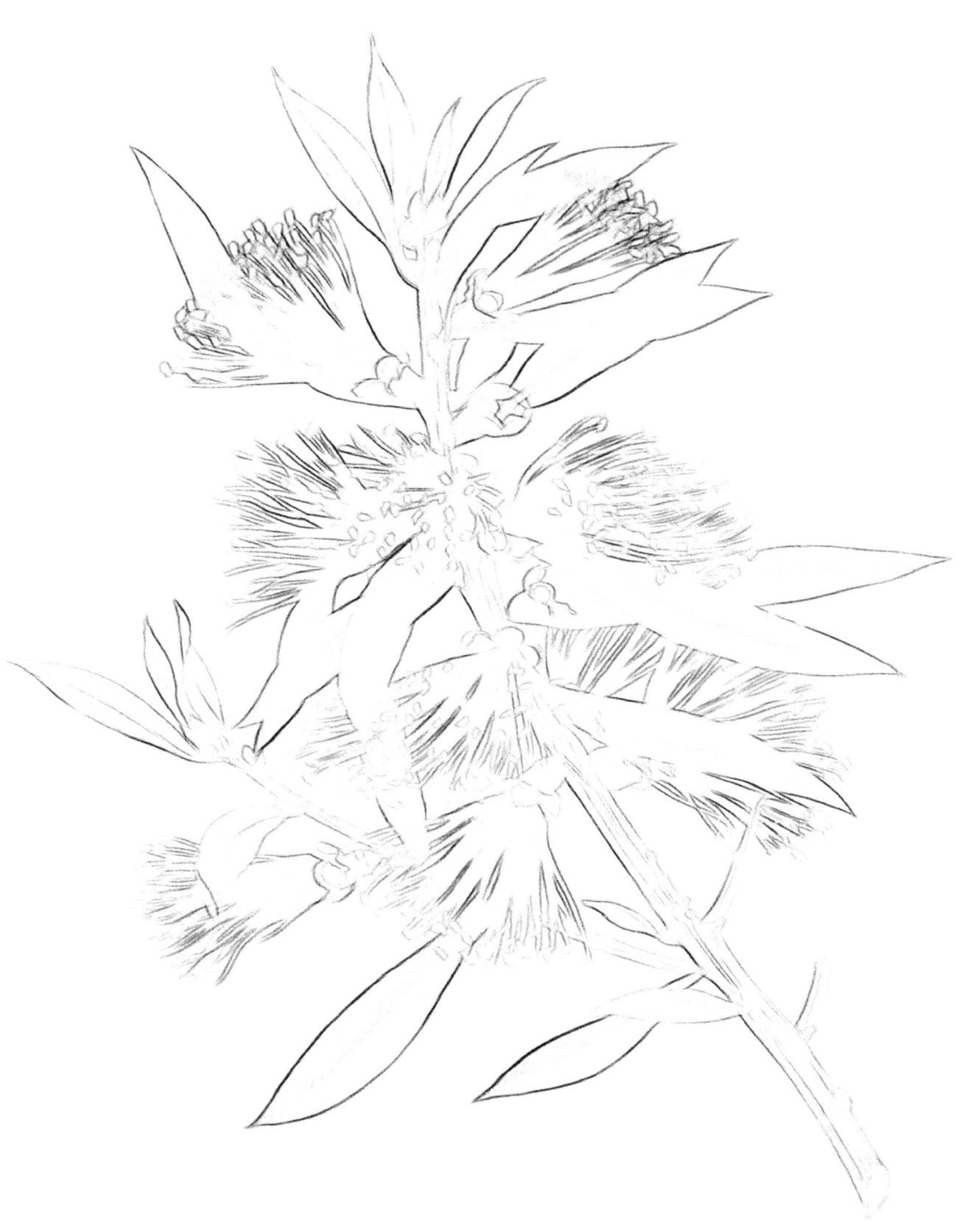

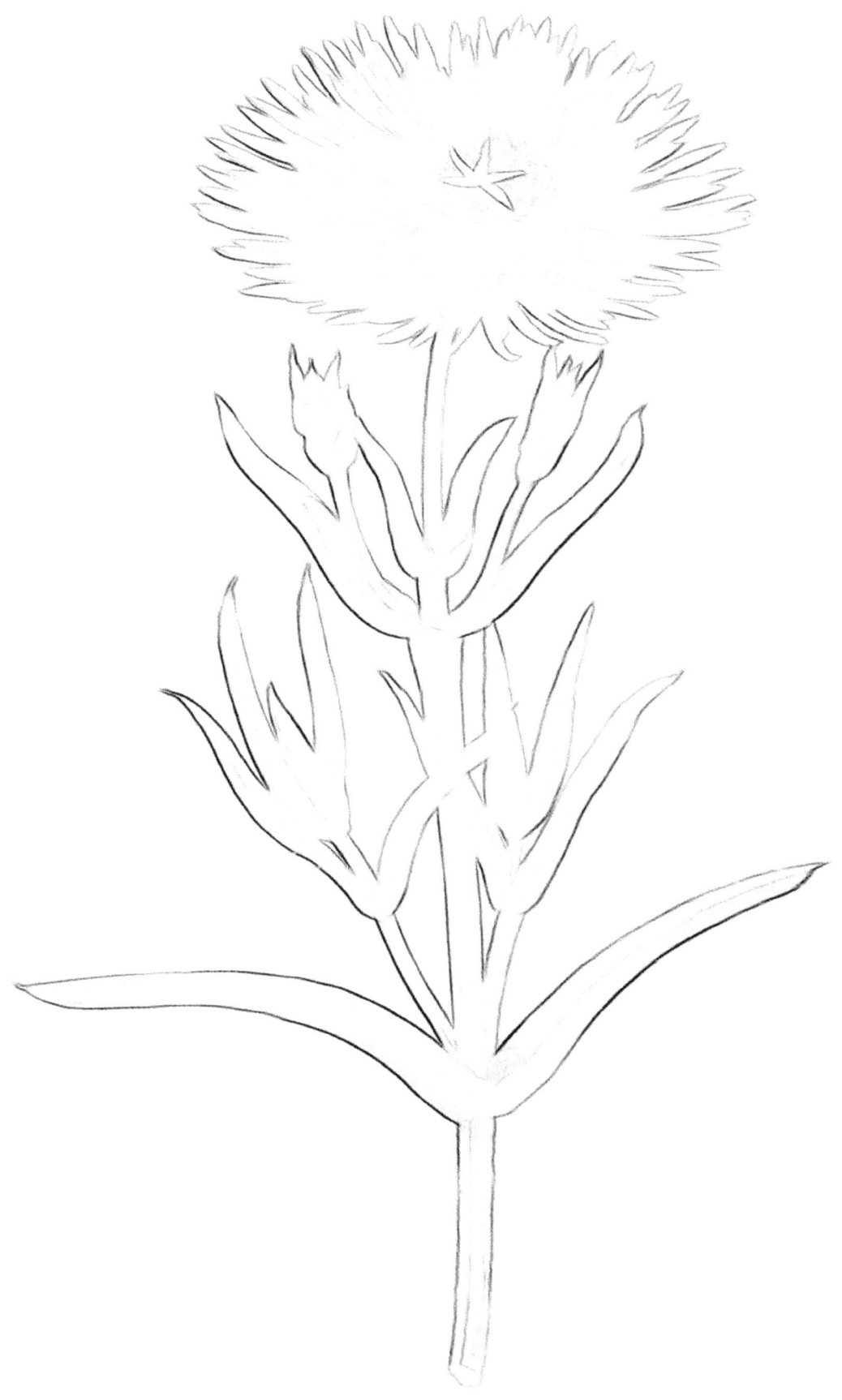

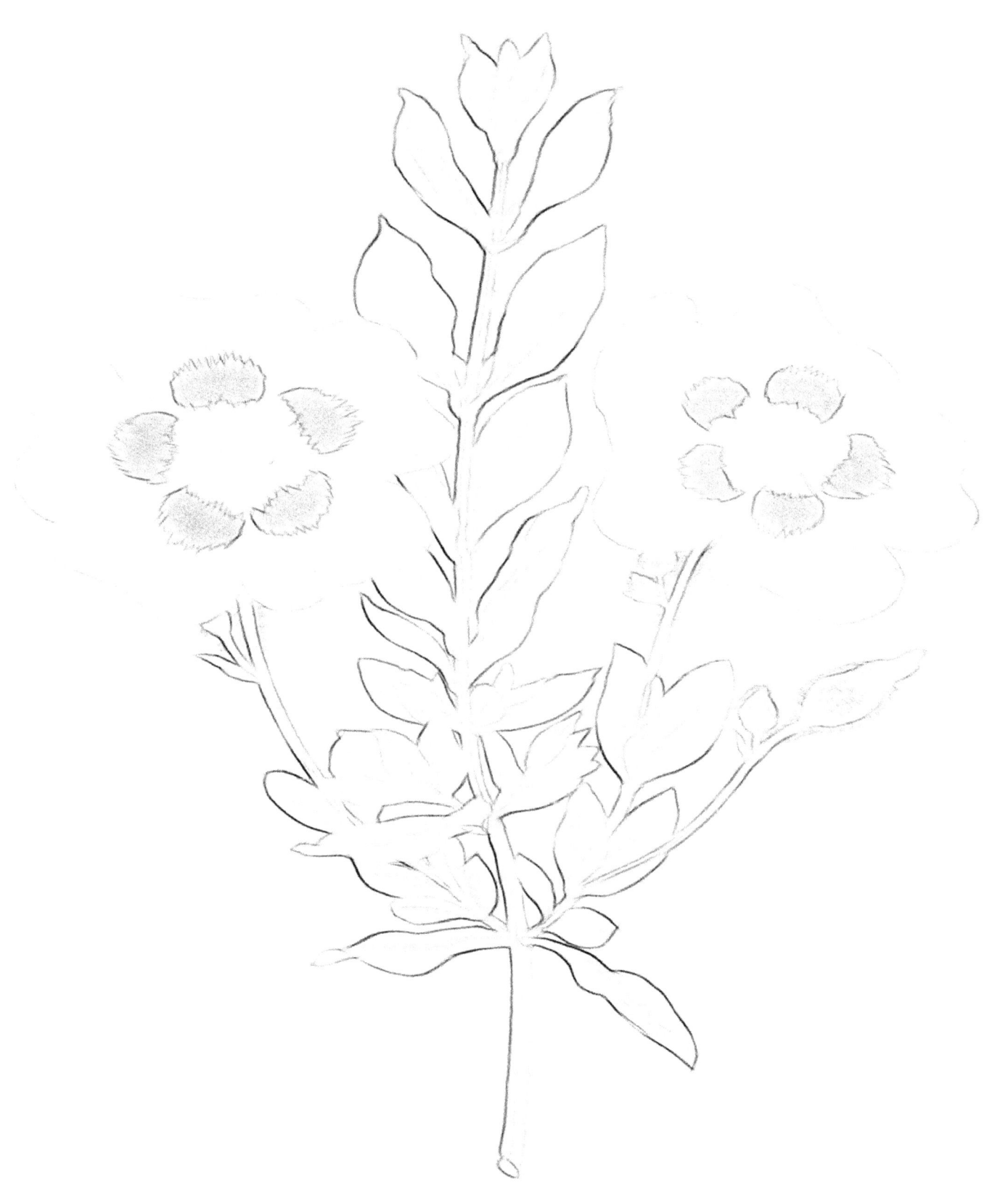

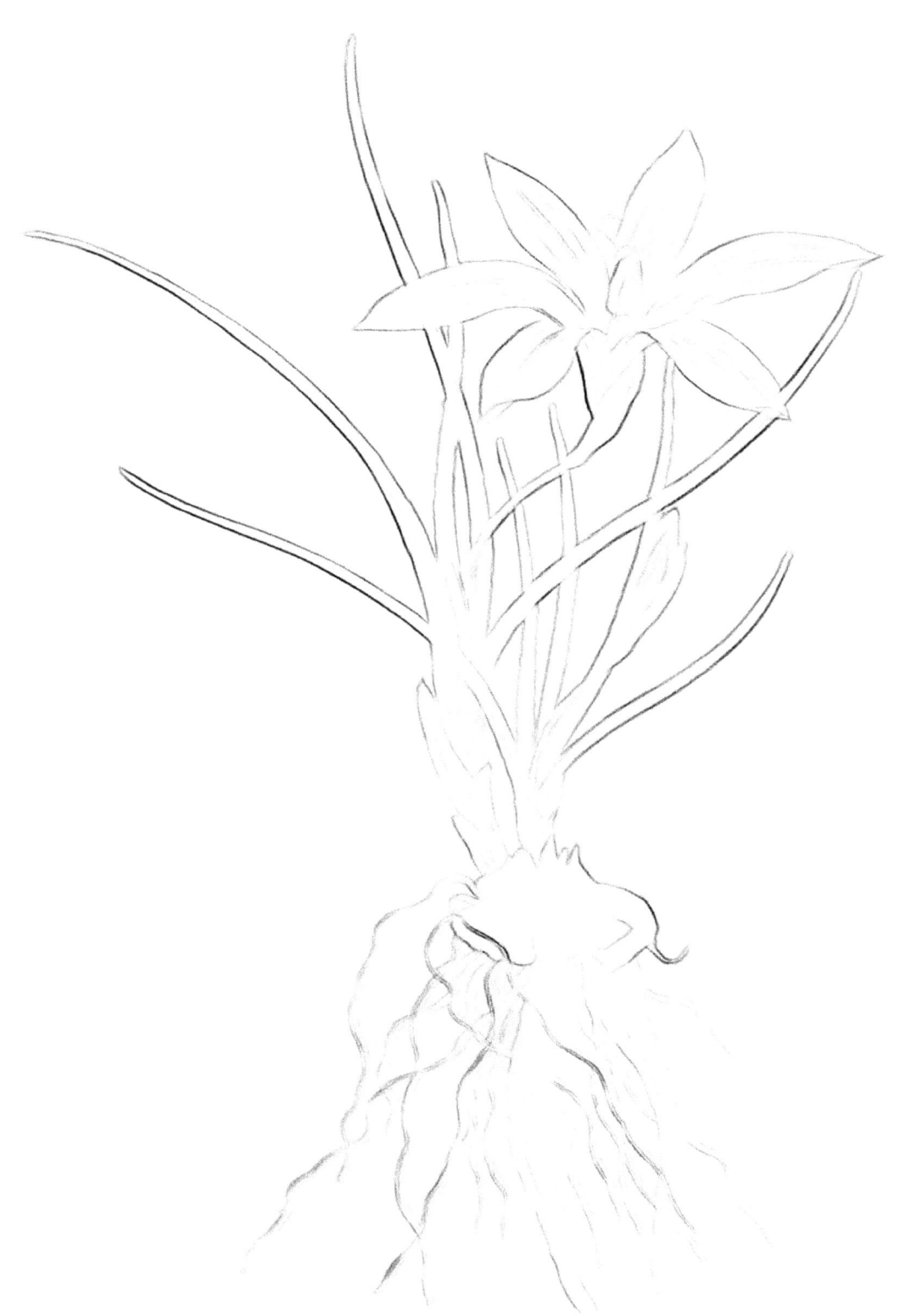

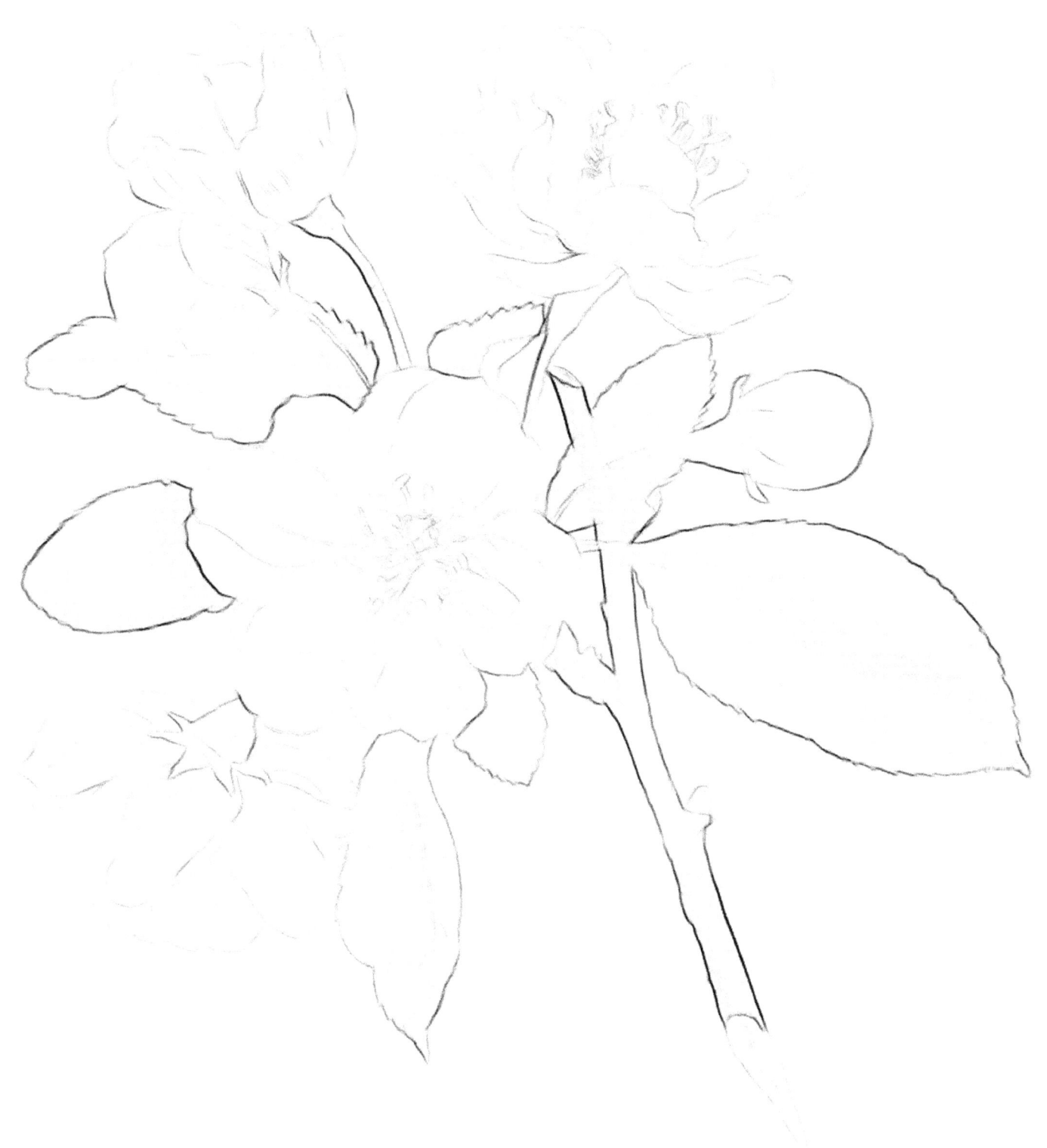

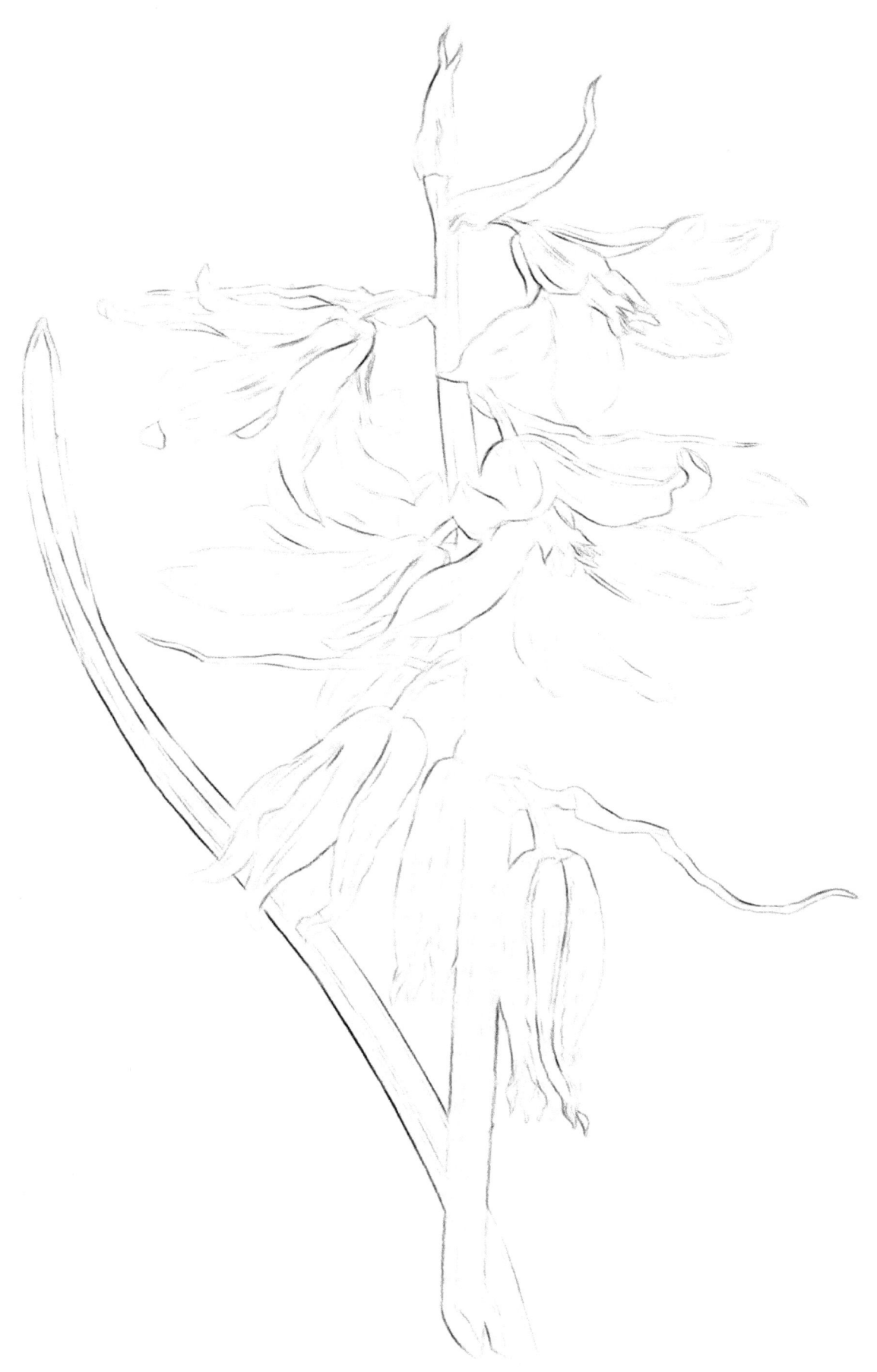